WINCHESTER
CONNECTICUT

T0400194

WINCHESTER
CONNECTICUT

· A HISTORY *from* FOUNDING *to* FLOOD ·

VIRGINIA SHULTZ-CHARETTE

THE
History
PRESS

Published by The History Press
Charleston, SC
www.historypress.com

First published 2021

Manufactured in the United States

ISBN 9781467144162

Library of Congress Control Number: 2021934318

This book is dedicated to all the past, present and future residents of my beloved, adopted town.

CONTENTS

ACKNOWLEDGEMENTS

Special thanks to my husband, Joe, and son, Michael, who understood that when my door was closed, it meant "Do not disturb."

A great many thanks for the patience shown by my acquisitions editor, Mike Kinsella, who was very understanding about the length of time needed for this project.

To the many people who encouraged me, from the Soldiers' Monument Commission to the mayor, several selectmen and friends who are "boosters" of my work and kept me going when I hit a difficult patch, many thanks to all.

There are also many who contributed to my work. The Brooks-Greenwood chapter of the Daughters of the American Revolution gave me the names of all the men from Torrington and Winchester who participated in the Revolutionary War. It confirmed my belief that the men did not flee to the western lands to avoid service in the militias, as had often been reported. Charlene LaVoie gave me information on Ruth Cross's Edendale and a blueprint of the magnificent landscape. Henry Pond, upon my asking if I could take a photo of his 1793 house built by Abijah Wilson, not only gave permission but also gave me a tour of the two-century-old house! Then there was Sherry and Mike Connell, who gave me what they thought were 8x11 photographs of the 1955 flood, but upon investigation, Verna Gilson and I discovered that they were actually the more rare photographs in Winsted of the 1938 flood—I have now turned them over to the Beardsley Library's local history room. The website Ancestry.com is also a good hunting ground for research if you are very careful—Jean Moore and David Moore are the historians of the Alfred Moore family, and their research guided me to the *Century Magazine* that had articles by businessman/balloonist Alfred Moore and his friend, photographer John Doughty. Eureka! I also messaged Louis Cornelio, who discussed the Cornelio legacy with me. Great fun! I hope that some eager young historian will explore the world of the Italian Americans and other immigrant groups and their influence on Winsted. And I cannot forget John Banks, with whom I had the pleasure of sharing research regarding Cornelius Dayton when he was writing his book. In return, he shared Dayton's pension file with me. He made sure to credit me in his acknowledgements, and I am privileged to do the same with him. The generosity of these contributors has enriched this work.

And then there was Verna Gilson, the genealogist and local historian who runs the local history room at the Beardsley Library. When I was too sick to work, she looked up information for me, brought me books and articles and fulfilled every request I made. It is not an overstatement to say that the completion of this work rests on her shoulders as much as mine. Thank you, dear friend!

Chapter 1

ANDROS, THE CONNECTICUT CHARTER...AND JOHN BOYD

Captain Thomas Bull watched as two armed sloops approached Saybrook Fort. The ships had been sitting in the harbor for three days before a message was sent ashore demanding the fort and the town surrender. Bull had always thought that it would be New Amsterdam that would attempt to wrest control of Connecticut Colony land west of the Connecticut River, but the Dutch had given up their claim in 1650. Fourteen years later, the Dutch gave up New Amsterdam as well, after ceding the land to England in the Treaty of Westminster, which ended the Third-Anglo Dutch War. Ships bearing English soldiers sailed into the renamed New York not long after the Dutch soldiers sailed out. Now it was the king's brother, the Duke of York, whose emissary, Governor Edmund Andros of New York, threatened those very lands that the Dutch once coveted. And on July 12, 1675, Andros came ashore to claim the land for the Royal Duke.[1]

The Connecticut Colony had been founded in 1631 on the Warwick Patent, which merely transferred land from the Earl of Warwick but did not grant authority to establish government. Once the British monarchy was reestablished on the throne of England, after the death of Lord Protector Oliver Cromwell, the colony decided to get an official charter directly from King Charles II in order to protect its claims and its self-government as established under the Fundamental Orders of Connecticut (1639). Governor Jonathan Winthrop the Younger, whose grandfather had received a signet ring from Charles I, was sent on the mission. This personable emissary brought with him the executed king's ring to return to the son as a token of esteem for the new monarch. This may have clinched the deal. The Connecticut Charter of 1662 listed the colony's boundaries: its land lay west of the Narragansett, south of Massachusetts and as far as the South Sea (Pacific Ocean). It also included the New Haven Colony, much to the chagrin of that colony's leaders. Importantly, it allowed the colony to self-govern.[2]

But Charles II, the so-called Merry Monarch, in 1664 also gave a patent to his brother, James Stuart, the Duke of York, which appeared to include some of the same land he had previously given to the Connecticut Colony. Why the pleasure-loving libertine would encroach on the rights of the colonies after giving them legal recognition may be due to a lack of interest or knowledge of the geography of the colonies in the New World. Or it may have been a willingness to please the courtiers who surrounded him looking for his favors, including his brother, without thinking of the consequences. Letters from Connecticut followed, but the king, never answering the colonists, gave them room to claim that their charter was still valid.[3]

Winthrop and his deputy governor, William Leete, the former governor of the New Haven Colony, carefully picked their way through this minefield, but when they heard that Andros was using the excuse of the widespread Native American uprising, King Philip's War, to wend his way to Connecticut to supposedly "help" with security, Captain Thomas Bull was given orders to march his militia to protect the fort and the colony from a takeover by Andros. Captain Bull's order, from the deputy governor, was to treat Governor Andros with all due courtesy but to resist an attempt to take over the fort. "You are, in his Majesty's name, required to avoid striking the first blow, but if they begin, you are to defend yourselves, and do your best to secure his Majesty's interest and the peace of the whole Colony."[4]

Once Andros arrived at the fort, he directed his secretary to read the document that awarded him authority of all the land west of the Connecticut River—including Hartford. Captain Bull ordered the secretary to desist. Bull's men moved aside and refused to listen; instead, their protest was read to Andros's men. An enraged Andros insisted on leaving, and true to their orders, Bull's men courteously formed "a guard of honor" that marched the angry company to the water. When the ships passed the fort, both Andros and Bull, true to ritual, fired their cannons in a salute as both flew His Majesty's colors. Bloodshed was avoided.[5]

This was not the end of the matter. Andros and the Duke of York bided their time. More than ten years later, upon the death of Charles II in 1685, his brother and heir, James II, formerly the Duke of York, assumed the throne. Connecticut quickly moved to defend itself. On January 6, 1686, the western lands of the colony were divided and distributed to various towns. A footnote in the compilation of the records explained the rationale:

> *The General Court, in anticipation of the loss of the charter by a judgement on the Quo Warranto, or of being compelled to surrender it to Andros, now took such measures as were in their power to secure the colony against the future extraction of an arbitrary governor. The charter was yet valid and the governor and company were empowered to dispose of all vacant lands.*[6]

Letters once again were sent by messenger between Andros and the recently elected governor Robert Treat demanding all of the colony to submit to his authority. The goal was to form a Dominion of New England under the administration of Andros. The Connecticut Court carefully worded its missive stating that the British subjects were honor bound to abide by the king's decision but encouraged His Majesty to consider the amount of sacrifice of blood and treasure of the colonists in order to plant the flag of England in Connecticut. However, their pleas were in vain.[7]

Upon James II's ascension to the throne, his emissary came to Hartford in 1686 with a writ that "His Majesty intends to bring all New England under one government; and nothing is now remaining on your part, but to think of an humble submission and dutiful resignation of your charter." He threatened the colony that if it contested the decision, it would lose Connecticut to New York. He concluded, "Sirs, bless not yourselves with vain expectation of advantage and spinning out of time by delay."[8]

But delay Connecticut did. Meanwhile, Andros arrived in Boston bearing his commission as governor-general of New England and took over the government in the Massachusetts Bay Colony. Connecticut saw the writing on the wall and requested that if it had to join the confederation of New England to please unite it with Massachusetts. Andros mistakenly thought that Connecticut had surrendered. But he waited in vain for Connecticut to bear him its charter. At last, Andros realized that he would have to go to Hartford himself if he wanted to gain possession of the document. In the last days of October 1687, Andros arrived in Hartford.[9]

According to legend, the colony's leaders and Andros met at an inn (possibly situated where the Old State House now resides), owned by Zachariah Sandford, the official innkeeper of the colony. His inn, known as the Bunch of Grapes, was used as the meeting place for the legislative body of the colony, general court sessions and other public functions. Andros demanded the charter, but Governor Treat resisted. The debate continued into the evening, when candles were lit. The governor had the box containing the charter brought into the room and placed on the table before them. The candles, mysteriously, were extinguished. The charter—again, according to legend—was handed through an open window to Captain Joseph Wadsworth standing below. Wadsworth quickly brought it to a "noble oak-tree" standing near the entrance gate of late Governor Wyllys's mansion and hid it in the hollow of the ancient tree.[10]

Nevertheless, Andros still took over the government of Connecticut, although he definitely left charter-less. Yet former governor Robert Treat, as part of the deal struck, was placed on Andros's council, which enabled him to "exercise a quiet but thoughtful influence that proved a source of protection to his fellow-citizens."[11]

Fortunately for the colonies, the Dominion of New England was short-lived. It has often been said that since the invasion of the Normans in 1066, England has never again been invaded. However, in November 1688, the Dutch Stadholder, William III, Prince of Orange, who was James's nephew and son-in-law, invaded with a Dutch fleet and army. This was accomplished with the acknowledgement and encouragement of the English Parliament. William III and his wife, Mary II (James II's daughter), jointly ascended the throne of England in the bloodless Glorious Revolution.

The joy in New England cannot be overstated. On April 18, 1689, the colonists of Boston arrested Dominion officials and Andros. Ten months of captivity, including a period of solitary confinement after Andros's attempted escape to Rhode Island, concluded in the former governor's deportation back to England, where he was freed. Meanwhile, most of the colonies picked up where they had left off before the Dominion was formed. In Connecticut, Governor Treat resumed his office, and life returned to normal.[12]

Although some scholars dispute the "legend" of the mysterious disappearance of the Connecticut Charter and the Charter Oak story, there are some interesting facts that have emerged over the past two centuries. A trunk of letters, documents and a memoir were discovered by the prominent art collector Daniel Wadsworth, who founded the Wadsworth Atheneum in Hartford. Wadsworth was a descendant of Joseph Wadsworth, involved in the Charter Oak intrigue. The memoir described himself as the person who placed the charter in the oak tree on the Wyllys property. This was done, according to Joseph Wadsworth, per the request of Mrs. Wyllys, who was afraid to have the document found in her house. The memoir states that the duplicate, not the original charter, was placed in the tree—that the original had been sent to the southern part of the colony for safekeeping prior to Andros's arrival. If this is correct, the original must have been returned to the Wyllyses at some later date because a future investigation found that what was once thought to be the original charter was the duplicate.[13]

Here is the story, according to the February 17, 1903 edition of the *Winsted Evening Citizen*:

> *In the Colonial records of Connecticut it is stated how that in 1817 or 1818, while Mr. Boyd was preparing for college at the Hartford Grammar School, he boarded in the family of Rev. Dr. Flint of the South Church. Coming in one day from school, he noticed on the workstand* [sic] *of Mrs. Bissell, the doctor's mother-in-law, a dingy piece of parchment, covered on one side with black letter manuscript. In answer to his inquiries, Mrs. Bissell told him that having occasion for some pasteboard, her friend and neighbor, Mrs. Wyllys had sent her this. Mr. Boyd proposed to procure her a piece of pasteboard in exchange for the parchment, to which Mrs. Bissell consented. It was not, however, until six or eight years had elapsed when Mr. Boyd examined the parchment with care, when he learned for the first time what he thought (and was generally thought) until recently, was a duplicate of the charter.*

The *Colonial Record*, volume 4, published in 1868, states:

> *The original charter, which now hangs in the secretary's office at Hartford, is engraved on three skins. The duplicate was written on two. So much of the duplicate as remains being about threefourths* [sic] *of the second skin, is now in the library of the Connecticut Historical Society, where it was placed by the Hon. John Boyd, late secretary of state.*
>
> *Not long ago, however, search was made through the records in London, and it was found that five pounds was the fee paid for drafting the original charter and 20 shillings (one pound) for the duplicate. Examination of the documents showed that 20 shillings was written (probably a memoriam) on the supposed original charter and five pounds on the supposed duplicate so that now it is certain that the one saved by Mr. Boyd was the original and the one that hung for years in the secretary's office and has recently been hung in the state library is the duplicate. The Mrs. Wyllys spoken of was related to the former secretary of state by that name and the parchment was probably found in his effects.*[14]

John Boyd served Winchester in various public capacities, including twenty-six years as town clerk and three years as secretary of the State of Connecticut. *Beardsley Library.*

John Boyd—industrialist, town clerk, secretary of the State of Connecticut and author of *Annals and Family Records of Winchester, Conn.*, published in 1873—lived in one of the towns saved, in January 1686, by royal order from possible annexation to New York. Boyd never knew that he had in his possession the original Connecticut Charter.

Chapter 2

THE "OLD SOCIETY" AND THE "NEW SOCIETY"

SETTLEMENT AND FOUNDING

Surprisingly, there was no haste made to survey and settle the western vacant lands of the colony after the restoration of self-government in 1690. Several decades passed before action was taken. Litchfield was incorporated as a town at the insistence of Hartford and Windsor in 1719. However, Windsor and Hartford were warned that the colony would not open the remaining lands for settlement. "That the whole of said tract of land shall lie for the further dispose of this Assembly; and all surveyors and persons appointed to lay out lands are hereby forbidden to bound or lay out any of said land without the special order of this Assembly."[15]

No patent had been given them in 1686; therefore, the opinion of the General Court was that the lands were held by the two towns only while the threat of Andros remained viable. The towns were expected to willingly hand back the lands after the threat was over. Windsor and Hartford did not quite see the topic as settled.

The colonial government spent much of its time, at this juncture, delineating land boundaries with New York (again), Massachusetts and Rhode Island, as well as settling disputes of town lines within the colony. One land dispute in 1722 in the eastern portion of the state resulted in the arrest and incarceration of an individual that led to a riot and a jailbreak in Hartford. Although this disagreement had nothing to do with the western lands, the threats of draconian punishments to all who interfered with the colony's laws, especially those that pertained to the crime of "trespass," were designed to stop immigration to the vacant western lands. Death or impossibly high fines could be the result.[16]

This did not stop the more intrepid in Windsor and Hartford. "This Assembly being informed that, notwithstanding the act of this Assembly… some persons, and particularly John Seymor, Samuel Catling and William Baker, of Hartford, and Thomas More and Job Elseworth, of Windsor, have been so hardy as to adventure, without the leave of this Assembly, presumptuously and in defiance of the said act, to lay out a township in the Colonies lands north of Litchfield." The court ordered the attorney for the county of New Haven to prosecute these persons once arrested. The temper in the towns of Windsor and Hartford escalated, and in the latter half of 1723, to avoid conflict, the Assembly adjusted its tone and started work on a compromise.[17]

The proposed compromise in 1726 equally divided the vacant lands between the colony, Windsor and Hartford. The colony would have the eastern side and the towns the western side. The Assembly promised a patent under the seal of the colony to both towns. Windsor and Hartford took their time but eventually agreed to the deal in 1729.[18]

After surveying in 1732, the two towns made their divisions of the land received in their patents. Hartford received Winchester, Hartland, New Hartford and the eastern portion of Harwinton. Windsor received Barkhamsted, Colebrook, Torrington and the western portion of Harwinton.[19]

Hartford and Windsor determined to give lands to their taxpayers, using the 1720 tax rolls to determine the size of their allotments. In 1744, Winchester's names were revealed, and years later, in 1763, the lots that had previously been laid out were distributed to the proprietors or their heirs. All were entitled to land in the three divisions. The lots were long and narrow, not conducive to farming and difficult to sell. Less well-off proprietors received "driblets." Joseph Root, whose tax bill in 1720 was one pound, received his land as follows: in the first and second division, he received strips one mile long and 8.25 feet wide. In the third division, he received a strip a half mile long and 16.5 feet wide, which in total gave him the three acres he was entitled. The wealthy held on to their lots in hopes that prices would rise. None of the proprietors ever settled in Winchester.[20]

Prior to the division, Caleb Beach of Goshen purchased land in the southwest corner of the town just over the Goshen line and half a mile north of Torrington, known as Hall Meadow, and erected the first dwelling in 1750. By 1756, he had sold all his land and moved back to Goshen, where he died a few years later. As a window into the world of the mid-eighteenth-century farmer, Beach's will left to various members of his immediate family these items: four chests, a bed, a great spinning-wheel, a double spinning-wheel, plough irons and drag teeth with plow chains, three steel traps, a shaving knife, a table, pewter platters, pewter plates, pewter basins, pewter porringers, one pair of tongs, one fire shovel, one trammel, one pair of andirons, one brass warming pan, one brass skillet, a brass kettle, one iron kettle and three iron pots. The recipient of the "three steel traps and shaving knife" was his son Joel.[21]

Joel Beach was about fifteen years old when the family moved to Winchester. When the family moved back to Goshen, he remained for a year and then moved to Torrington until 1761. He then returned to Winchester and lived on Blue Street, a little south of where the old stone school was built in the nineteenth century. A giant of a man at nearly six feet, five inches, this mighty hunter never failed to catch his prey, and he usually dined on bear meat, venison and wild turkey. Either his first wife, Abiah Filley, or his second, Amy Johnson, was no mean shot with a musket herself. It is told that a panther was in the tree in her yard, and since Joel was away from home at the time, she picked up the musket and killed the varmint with a bullet to the brain. A frontier woman could not afford to have die-away airs![22]

At about the same time that Joel Beach moved into town, William Filley of Torrington bought land in Hall Meadow that included the land and house previously occupied by Caleb Beach. The house was torn down around 1770. It is possible that what is memorialized as the Caleb Beach chimney became part of the dwelling erected by Filley. Filley drowned at the age of thirty-nine in 1774.[23]

Landlord Adam Mott from Windsor operated a tavern in 1754 on a bridle-path that became the Old South Road. This was located across from where the Hurlbut Cemetery now resides. The walls were of unhewn logs, with a rustic roof of hemlock bark. It is unclear how he could maintain a tavern other than for the occasional hunter to clear his throat with a taste of the contents of a keg of rum. In 1761, he sold the tavern to his three sons and went back to Windsor, where he died.[24]

Lack of roads through much of Winchester, especially the northern sector, made the town inaccessible and undesirable for many. And yet roads, or at least bridle-paths, were needed for settlers to pass through to more fertile lands in Canaan and Goshen, as well as to the mining industry started in the 1730s in Salisbury. There were some passable roads in the upland pastures of Winchester, located in the southern portion of

Often mistaken as the Caleb Beach House, which was a log house removed in 1770, this is the Filley House, built on the same spot in Hall Meadow. *Author's postcard collection.*

the town, that allowed settlers to move in or pass through via Torrington, Goshen or Norfolk, but the northern area had to be cleared by axe and backbreaking work.[25]

In the northwestern quadrant of the town, the General Assembly in 1758 addressed this lack and insisted that a more convenient road be established to make way for carriages and, in time of war, for men marching. A possible roadway was proposed, and in May 1760, it was ordered that the way be cleared and made passable for traveling before November 20, 1761. Towns and proprietors were responsible for the work, and in case of noncompliance, road crews would be hired at the expense of the delinquents. This road would be known as the North Road. There were only a few families in Winchester, so payment was made by land grants in the southern portion of the town. According to Winchester resident and historian John Boyd, "It was a wonder of the age that a direct and practicable route of steep rocky hills and mountains of the Green Woods for travel, and soon became…the sole thoroughfare of the colony in the direction of Albany." Boyd cautioned that the road was no "Appian Way": "Direct as it was, it went up and down the highest hills, on uneven beds of rocks and stones, and passed marshy valleys on corduroy of the coarsest hemlock log texture." In Winchester, it went over Wallen's Hill and down to the Still River near the Abijah Wilson Jr. homestead and then up Dishmill Hill and onward by the Rowley Pond to Colebrook.[26]

Hurlbut Cemetery, established in the mid-nineteenth century, is located on South Road, possibly on the site of John Hills gun shop and across the road from the first tavern. *Author's photo collection*.

The Abijah Wilson House, located near the Old North Road. He arrived in Winsted and built his house in 1793. He served seven terms as selectman. *Author's photo collection*.

Just south of the Wilson homestead lived John Balcom Jr., who came from Mansfield to Winsted via the North Road. He owned a lot east of the Still River on which he built a log house just slightly north of the present-day Route 8 and 20 junction. Balcom was the brother of Elias Balcom, who ran a sawmill until his death in Winsted in 1776; they probably shared their homestead and were in the business together.[27]

John Balcom Jr. was involved in founding the Congregational Church in Winsted; the first item on his probated inventory was his Bible. He definitely took his religion seriously, grabbing Ethan Allen's horse's reins in an attempt to arrest Allen for breaking the Sabbath. Allen prevailed by drawing his sword with a threat and a curse that sent Balcom scurrying back to the safety of his house. Balcom died in Winchester in 1808, leaving two large plots of land near the Still River. Balcom's probated will was considerably longer than that of Joel Beach, which indicates some success in his lifetime.[28]

Just prior to the time when John Balcom moved into what is now Winsted, David Austin purchased land in Winchester. In 1769, he extended his holdings down to Winsted between the Lake Street bridge and Case Avenue. This required the backbreaking job of hacking through the jungle-like brush, brambles and timber from the highland pastures of Winchester, down past Long Pond (Highland Lake) to the "howling wilderness" of Winsted. On Lake Street, almost opposite from Rockwell Street, Austin built the first gristmill in 1771 and a sawmill. This would be the southern terminus until the Greenwoods Turnpike was built near the end of the century. Austin moved his family to Vermont in 1796.[29]

Meanwhile, the family of Benoni Hills began to move into Winchester, ultimately becoming a major factor in ecclesiastical, military and political affairs. Hills was born circa 1700 in Glastonbury. As a youth, he went to Northampton to apprentice with the Pomeroy family, of whom, at that time, Medad Pomeroy was the patriarch. There he learned the craft of ironmaking, particularly gun-making.[30]

Hills and his wife, Hannah Strong Hills, had eleven children. The first was born in Suffield. The next eight were born in Durham, and the last two children were born in Goshen in 1741 and 1743. Several of this progeny would eventually move to Winchester at a very propitious time.

First would be Seth Hills, who in 1765 was granted a deed of fifty acres near the Torrington line in Winchester in 1765. Mr. Hills was first deacon of the church, and first representative of the town; "a man of hardy constitution, indomitable energy, sound good sense, and sincere piety; his integrity without a stain."[31]

John Hills arrived in Winchester prior to 1767 and established on his farm a gun shop, either on or near the Hurlbut Cemetery on South Road. It is less clear when another son, Colonel Medad Hills (probably named after Medad Pomeroy, who taught Benoni the craft), came to Winchester, where he was a large landowner, although he lived much of his life and died in Goshen on the Torrington line. Medad was involved in contractual arms production with the state. On February 24, 1776, Colonel Charles Burd acknowledged receipt of ten muskets with bayonets and belts made by Hills.[32]

Medad Hills had been involved with the local militia in Goshen since 1769, and after the outbreak of the war, he was elected captain in the local militia, which consisted of men from Goshen, Torrington and Winchester. He was soon promoted to major and then colonel. John was appointed lieutenant of the trainband in Winchester in 1775 by the General Assembly; in 1776, he was appointed captain of the Twelfth Company in the Seventeenth Regiment. For the year of 1778, he was appointed captain of a company wholly comprising Winchester men and may have been involved in 1779 in driving out Governor Tryon's invasion of Connecticut. But by 1780, the war had moved south, and he is thought to have returned to his gun-making with his father and brother.[33]

Another son, Beriah, came to Winchester in 1769 and lived on the Torrington line. He was appointed "to read the psalms" at the old meetinghouse. He died in 1778 and is buried at Winchester Cemetery near his father.[34] Benoni and sons John, Seth and Beriah were instrumental in the founding of Winchester.

A petition to the General Assembly dated August 4, 1767, was presented to the statehouse in New Haven (at that time Hartford and New Haven alternated the meetings of the General Assembly; Connecticut in effect had two state capitals). The petition asked the assembly to "incorporate and form us into a town with town privileges, and lay a small tax on all the divided lands in said township…lying south and west of Long Pond." Seth Hills was the first signatory, and John and Beriah also signed. Winchester was allowed to tax residents to support the church founded in this Ecclesiastical Society, but no mention was made of allowing a township to be incorporated. Seth Hills was voted clerk and deacon for the society.[35]

In March 1771, it was voted to petition the Assembly for a town corporation in a memorial written by Seth and John Hills, inhabitants of the Ecclesiastical Society, established in the township of Winchester. They asked to incorporate the township and enable them to tax owners of lands (proprietors), in addition to residents, to support the church and schools.

Benoni Hills's self-carved gravestone at the Old Burying Grounds on South Road. He was a prominent gunsmith who taught his sons the trade. *Author's photo collection.*

Beriah and Benoni Hills also signed. The General Assembly agreed in May 1771. Therefore, Benoni and sons Beriah, John and Seth Hills were among the original founders of the Town of Winchester. Yet few of this influential family remained in Winchester.[36]

Although Seth Hills was the first representative of Winchester to the General Assembly, he nevertheless cleared land in Vernon, Oneida County, New York, in 1798 and moved his family there in 1799. Captain John Hills sold his homestead at the close of the war in 1781 and moved to Charlotte, Vermont, where he continued his gun-making trade. It can be assumed that this is when Medad moved back to Goshen.[37]

Benoni moved to Torrington but eventually came back to Winchester, bringing with him two headstones that he had carved on mica slate. One read, "Benoni Hills, this is my house," and the other, which is still partially readable, stated, "O eternity, death is come"; after his death, it was added, "June 24, 1793."[38]

Chapter 3

"'TIS TIME TO PART"

THE AMERICAN REVOLUTION

While Winchester was establishing itself as a town in the remote region of Connecticut, Great Britain was tightening its grip on its colonies. As a result of the British and American victory in the French and Indian War (1756–63), the mother country was faced with a hefty price tag. This cost, according to the British Exchequer, should not be borne by Britain alone. A series of unpopular taxes was introduced by Parliament, to be paid by colonists, without representation, to pay down the debt.

Colonial Connecticut and Rhode Island were the only two colonies not governed by proprietors or by a royal governor. The Stamp Act (1765) infuriated most colonists, but it was the eastern portion of the Connecticut Colony that was most willing to resist. The governor, Thomas Fitch IV, sided with the more measured western portion of the colony, whose residents feared that resistance would result in losing the charter, which had been repeatedly threatened in the past, and would once again put the western portion of the colony in danger of being absorbed by New York. Governor Fitch's willingness to comply with the Stamp Act resulted in Connecticut's Sons of Liberty manipulating the 1766 election in favor of William Pitkin of Hartford for governor and Jonathan Trumbull of Lebanon as deputy governor.[39]

Although Great Britain rescinded the Stamp Act, it issued a declaration that stated its right to impose its will on the subject colonies. In 1767, a series of acts known as the Townshend Acts, named after Chancellor of the Exchequer Charles Townshend, levied taxes on a long list of items, including china, glass, paint, paper and tea. Non-importation of these items was the road to resistance; nevertheless, Connecticut veered from the path at times since some of these items were sold by peddlers from royalist New York to customers in the southwest portion of Connecticut, where British sympathies were the strongest.[40]

Fortunately, Parliament was convinced to partially repeal the Townshend Acts, leaving only a tax on tea. But the Boston Tea Party (1773) ended what the British considered their indulgence of the colonies. Punitive laws took away self-governance in Massachusetts, and in 1774, the British closed the port of Boston. Connecticut realized that its colony's future hung in the balance as well.[41]

Jonathan Trumbull Sr., who became governor upon the death of Pitkin in 1769, sympathized with Boston, and after the action at Lexington and Concord in 1775, known as the "Lexington Alarm," Trumbull sent two conservative emissaries, as much to get them out of the way as to send a letter to the military governor of Massachusetts, General Thomas Gage. Trumbull secretly met with his colonial assembly to prepare for war and to send aid to the residents of Boston.[42]

According to John Boyd, author of the first history of the town of Winchester:

> *It is often said that the settlement of this and other neighboring towns was greatly accelerated by immigration of men of more prudence than courage or patriotism, who hoped in this remote region to escape from compulsory military service. If this is true, they found it a poor refuge for noncombatants, for it would be difficult to find an able-bodied man of that period who had not seen hard service, either as a volunteer or detached militiaman.*[43]

A few area men marched off to the aid of Boston almost immediately. Eli Andrus, Ebenezar Shepard and Charles Wright marched with Captain Seth Smith's Company of New Hartford. Charles Wright's brother, Freedom, who owned a tavern in Winchester near his father and brothers, joined with Captain Timothy Gaylord of Norfolk for the relief of Boston. However, the New Hartford company probably turned back since records credit it with three days' march—Gaylord's company marched five days. There were no provisions in Boston, and returning Connecticut men warned those coming to assist to turn back. For the most part, Litchfield County held back until the end of April while war preparations were made, answering the requests of Governor Trumbull for volunteers.[44]

Other men took it upon themselves to protect Boston from the threat of Canada and saw a way to procure military arms. Two Connecticut men, unknowingly, had the same idea at virtually the same time. Ethan Allen from Litchfield and Benedict Arnold from Norwich looked northwest to Fort Ticonderoga, once an essential outpost on the southern end of Lake Champlain. Allen, with support from other Patriots, rounded up his Green Mountain Boys and headed to the once great fortress. Arnold went to Massachusetts to get permission from the revolutionaries there. Ultimately, Allen and Arnold arrived almost at the same time. On May 10, 1775, they captured the fort without a fight.[45]

Immediately, Colonel Benjamin Hinman's Eighth Regiment was sent by Governor Trumbull to take over from Allen and Arnold. Allen and his men had already plundered the fort and left when the liquor ran out, but Arnold was still there, trying to ready the armaments to be shipped to Massachusetts. Arnold, to say the least, was not pleased that Hinman was sent to replace him in June and refused to serve under him, leaving when Massachusetts revolutionary leaders decided in favor of the Connecticut colonel.[46]

Hinman's regiment was a seven-month regiment and included men from Winchester. In Sedgewick's Eighth Company, his first lieutenant was a Winchester man: Warham Gibbs, the first moderator of Winchester's town meeting and a man respected for shouldering spiritual and secular duties. Also serving were Adam Mott Jr., David Goff, Peleg Sweet, Lemuel Walter and Noah Gleason Jr. Apparently, those men were able to stay until their enlistment was up. However, sickness, especially smallpox, was rife in the Northern District, and numerous men were discharged early. Stephen Arnold was discharged on September 2, as were Nathan Balcom, Ebenezar Shepard, Charles Wright, David Wright (erroneously listed in some books as having died on the march to the fort), William Stannard and Abraham Wilkinson. John Darbe and Freedom Wright left on September 4, Hawkins Woodruff left on September 11 and Elisha Smith was discharged on September 16. Oliver Coe Sr. was discharged on November 20 and on the way home fell ill with a fever. He brought the illness home to his wife and six young children, all of whom survived. However, Coe died on December 31 at the age of thirty-seven.[47]

Meanwhile, Charles Webb's Seventh Regiment also enlisted men from western Connecticut and was stationed at various points along Long Island Sound until September 14, 1775. George Washington ordered it to the Boston Camp to Winter Hill, to the left of the besieging line. There it remained until the expiration of its service in December. Winchester

Oliver Coe's gravestone. He sickened and died at home from disease contracted at Fort Ticonderoga, infecting his entire family. They survived. *Author's photo collection.*

men served in several companies of the regiment. Samuel Hurlbut, the progenitor of one of the most important families in Winchester, served in the Fifth Company along with John Sweet. John Wright (brother of Charles, David and Freedom) served in the Sixth Company, while Gideon Wilcoxson enlisted in the Tenth Company.[48]

Meanwhile, Burral's Regiment—after the disastrous loss at Quebec on December 31, 1775, that claimed the life of General Richard Montgomery, seriously injured Benedict Arnold, and made Ethan Allen a prisoner of war—was formed to aid the remaining battered and ill soldiers stationed outside Quebec's walls. Men who reenlisted from Winchester—Charles Wright, Adam Mott Jr., Eli Andrus and David Goff—hoped to lay siege to Quebec, but it proved ineffectual; the New Englanders had to head back to Ticonderoga in April 1776 ahead of the advancing British army.[49]

On March 17, 1776, the British realized that their position in Boston Harbor was untenable. The mission that Benedict Arnold had started, by capturing Ticonderoga and refurbishing and inventorying the military hardware, was completed by Henry Knox. Knox then brought cannons from the fort by hauling the artillery across frozen rivers and the Berkshire Mountains to the Boston siege camps. These cannons, mounted on Dorchester Heights, were a threat to the British navy in Boston Harbor. The British evacuated their army, carrying with them Massachusetts Royalists, and sailed to Nova Scotia.

Three months later, General William Howe sailed for New York with nine thousand men. German Hessians and other troops met with Howe's fleet when it arrived in New York, and Howe's brother, Admiral Lord Richard Howe, arrived shortly after. The British would land twenty-five thousand troops against the nineteen thousand troops of George Washington. Because Washington was unable to determine where the British were to land, he split his army between fortified positions on Long Island, Manhattan and mainland locations.[50]

While Howe was sailing toward New York, Governor Trumbull asked that his General Assembly instruct Connecticut delegates to the Continental Congress that the colonies press for a declaration of independence and a plan of union. They did so on June 15, 1776. While Howe was landing his troops on Staten Island on July 2, members of the Continental Congress were putting the finishing touches on the Declaration of Independence.[51]

On July 6, news reached New York that Congress had voted for independence. On Tuesday evening, July 9, Washington had several brigades march onto the commons of the city to hear the Declaration of Independence read. After the end of the reading, a mob ran down to Bowling Green Park with ropes and bars, where they tore down the gilded lead equestrian statue of King George III. The crowd cut off the statue's head and mounted the head on a spike outside a tavern, and the rest of the statue was dragged to Litchfield, Connecticut, where residents made musket balls.[52]

Due to a disastrous loss for the Americans, the British were convinced that the Americans would never face them again—the rebellion had surely been put down. They were wrong, but the Revolution was certainly at one of its low points. Desertion was rampant, Nathan Hale was hanged as a spy, the beleaguered Continentals continued to battle and they continued to lose. The battle at Fort Washington was the final blow in Washington's hope to keep a foothold in New York City.[53]

Captain Beebe's Litchfield Company under Wadsworth's Brigade had in its ranks four men from the town of Winchester: Gershom Fay, William Fay, Remembrance Filley and Gideon Wilcoxson. He was told to select a party of men to join in the defense of Fort Washington on the island of Manhattan. General Nathanael Greene had convinced Washington not to leave New

York but to try and hold on to the fort in order to keep abreast of British troop movements. Fortunately for the Fays or Filley, they were not chosen with Beebe to go with him and thirty-six other men. Wilcoxson was selected and was captured with the entire garrison when a Pennsylvania turncoat gave instructions on the fort's weaknesses. It was over very quickly. More than 2,800 prisoners were marched off to the notorious British prison ships, churches and sugar houses of New York on November 16, 1776.[54]

Captain Beebe, like most officers, was not treated gently, but he was able to move around the town. He tried to keep watch over his thirty-six men, but only six survived the abuse, the rancid food, the cold and the disease, particularly smallpox. On January 1, 1777, a boat of prisoners who were still alive when it left New York sailed for Milford and left men, dead and dying, on the shore. Wilcoxson was not among them. The state records did not ascertain if he was dead or if he lived. He must have been returned on a later ship, as church records in Shelton, Connecticut, state that he died on April 11, 1777, "after returning from captivity." He was twenty-five. More men died from the cruel abuse at the British prisons than died from military action in the entire war.[55]

European armies did not fight in the winter. This was to General George Washington's advantage and disadvantage. After the British chased Washington and his entourage into Pennsylvania, they decided not to press on, as winter weather was upon them. Washington's disadvantage was that, as in 1775, his army's enlistments were up in December since they, too, followed the British model.

Washington knew that he had to make a move quickly or he would lose his army and would not be able to raise another. He knew he needed a "brilliant stroke" to save the cause. His entourage included a light cavalry regiment from Connecticut. In Captain Seymour's company were two trumpeters from Winchester—Joseph Hoskin and Truman Gibbs—as well as private Roswell Coe. Their role was to accompany the troops to Washington's destination. Hoskin was discharged on November 29 and Gibbs on December 24 after reaching their destination on the west side of the Delaware River; Coe was discharged on December 26, after Washington crossed the Delaware.[56]

Although the plans did go somewhat awry, as two of the landings by other officers were impossible due to the northeaster that sprang up that evening, Washington was able to cross on Christmas Eve to make a surprise attack on the Hessian headquarters at Trenton, New Jersey, the next morning. About 2,400 men crossed with Washington on an ice-filled river during a blizzard. Boats carrying forty men standing and others carrying horses, cannons and military supplies made the trip without a mishap. Two of the men were from Winchester: Lieutenant Samuel Hurlbut and Sergeant Ozias Brownson, in what would be called Elisha Bostwick's Company (though at the time, he was the second lieutenant) in the Charles Webb Regiment.[57]

Upon arriving in Trenton, Henry Knox positioned the cannons at the heads of the main streets. When the Hessians poured out of the buildings, the cannons greeted them, driving them into the side streets and into the fire of the soldiers. It was all over in forty-five minutes. The only American fatalities were two men who froze to death on the march. Twenty-one Hessians were dead, including the mortally wounded Colonel Rall, who had been a commander at the Battle of Fort Washington. The Americans captured almost nine hundred prisoners. Here, then, was the "brilliant stroke."[58]

On December 30, 1776, the last day of enlistment, Washington asked his troops to reenlist. None responded. A few minutes later, he asked that they give him one more month. Sergeant Ozias Brownson did, as did many others. They marched to Princeton on January 3, 1777, where a quick battle raged from a farm to Nassau Hall, part of the College of New Jersey, now called Princeton University. The Americans again won, suffering casualties, but the British suffered more and three hundred were made prisoners.[59]

The year 1776 had shown that Great Britain had no intention of leaving, especially after its numerous victories in New York. The war would, as most wars do, take much longer to come to a conclusion than the populace expected. Therefore, in October 1776, the Continental Congress finally agreed with General Washington that a standing army was necessary for the successful conclusion of the war. Washington issued a call for eighty-eight regiments of 728 men each. Connecticut's portion of the levy was eight regiments.[60]

In the standing Continental army, enlistees could sign up for the duration of the war or three years. This would offer some hope of curtailing problems besetting the states. Shortages of supplies, particularly agricultural, would be reduced if communities could count on a core of farmers producing crops and livestock to feed, not only their own families and those whose men were off fighting but also the militias and the Continental army. Connecticut was considered the "Provision State," but entire crops were either unplanted or unharvested due to the continual call for more troops. It was hopeful that a well-trained, year-round army could have smaller regiments that were more efficient—that would allow some farmers to work on their agricultural duties without the constant need to pull them away.[61]

The constant disruption of the army and the state militias with short enlistments ranging from one month to a year made planning military campaigns and even providing guns and supplies difficult. Military strategy and tactics were often determined by when the enlistments of the regiments were due to expire. In addition, the army and the state rarely received the weapons (or any supplies) back from the soldiers when their current tour of duty was completed. Replacing weapons on a large scale was next to impossible, as guns were handcrafted. Even repairing the guns required a great deal of time, as parts had to be made as well.[62]

Nevertheless, calls for volunteers met with apathy. During the first few months, few Continental regiments could even muster more than eighty volunteers. In addition, state regiments and militia were in competition with the Continental army. Shorter enlistments in state regiments and militias allowed men to get crops planted and harvested, making state recruitment more attractive, but that did not mean that men were willing to sign up with the state either. This left Connecticut in dire straits, as Governor Trumbull could not fulfill the levies of the Continental army, nor did the Continental army have the manpower available to give Trumbull soldiers during a period when Connecticut was most vulnerable.

On December 1, 1776, General Howe sent his navy and soldiers to take Newport, Rhode Island. This meant that Connecticut was vulnerable to invasion from three sides: on the east from Rhode Island, the south along Long Island Sound and the west from New York. There were even rumors that General John Burgoyne in Canada might send troops down the Connecticut River and attack from the north.[63]

In December, a very nervous General Assembly passed a law that required all male persons ages sixteen to sixty not already enlisted to form "alarm" companies. Men were required to answer the call to arms at any moment when summoned. Governor Trumbull, upset with the slow pace of enlistments for Continental regiments, in March 1777 delegated the responsibility of enlisting men to every town. They were assigned quotas that had to be filled. This would aid the state's protection as well, since most regiments would be stationed nearby along the Connecticut Line in New York, which ran through the highlands on the eastern side of the Hudson River and could defend Connecticut's western border and the shoreline if not occupied with the British army in New York.[64]

The state's fears were well founded. As men in short-term enlistments in the state militias were in the process of marching off to Peekskill, New York, Royal Governor William Tryon sent two thousand British troops to Connecticut to destroy the supply depot in Danbury. This was an army larger than the one sent to destroy munitions in Lexington and Concord. It had, just the month before, destroyed the supplies at Peekskill. In Danbury, only fifty Continental soldiers and one hundred militia were in the area as word came that Tryon was on his way. The troops decided to remove whatever supplies they could out of Danbury instead of fighting impossible odds; nevertheless, the invaders captured five thousand barrels of provisions and most of the army's tents. After loading or destroying the supplies, the soldiers drank the looted rum, carousing through the streets of Danbury throughout the evening, while the populace hid in their homes in terror. The next day, the army, aware that Generals Benedict Arnold and David Wooster were on their way with six hundred men, set fire to Danbury, with the exception of the homes and businesses of Loyalists who had aided them.[65]

Prior to reaching Danbury, a few men, possibly in a Connecticut militia, were captured by the British and sent back to New York as prisoners of war. One, Peter Blackman, was from Winchester. Only records of casualties and the wages and bills paid regarding the "Danbury Alarm" survive. It is thought that Ozias Brownson—who had signed up for a few months' service as ensign in Captain Barnes's company in Hooker's Regiment, which was on its way or at Peekskill—might have been involved since Barnes received wages for his participation. Also, members of Captain Medad Hills's "alarm" company from the surrounding towns did participate in chasing the British back to their ships, although the list does not include Hills's name as being present. His men got to Danbury too late to battle the British, as they had just boarded their ships. Hills was promoted to lieutenant colonel in the Seventeenth Regiment. These minutemen-style companies that were expected to participate in safeguarding Connecticut are seldom recognized (Medad's brother John Hills had an alarm company in 1778 that included most of the able-bodied male residents in Winchester who were otherwise not currently enlisted). The Hills brothers may or may not have seen action, but undoubtedly the muskets they produced under contract for the state did.[66]

Throughout the summer, state regiments, not all full, were sent to guard the shoreline, the Rhode Island border and especially the Connecticut Line in New York under the purview of General Israel Putnam. Other fears were being realized. General Burgoyne was indeed on the march from Canada, expected to join up with General Barry St. Leger and General William Howe in a pincer movement to cut off New England from its southern allies. Burgoyne quickly took Ticonderoga but began the long journey through wilderness to meet up with the generals to the west and south. It did not happen. Benedict Arnold stopped St. Leger, who was forced to turn back; General Howe inexplicably decided to invade Philadelphia, home of the Continental Congress, rather than join forces with Burgoyne.

On October 4, Howe and his forces met in the first full-fledged European-style battle with Washington's troops outside Germantown, Pennsylvania. Although Washington's army did a credible job, they were hampered by a complicated plan, the resistance of one of the generals to the plan and a fog that hid friend and foe alike and resulted in a great deal of friendly fire. Howe won the day, but the troops were encouraged by their performance. Winchester was represented in the Fifth Regiment by Ebenezer Scoville. In the Seventh Regiment were John Walters and William Leach. Also joining them was fifteen-year-old Samuel Roberts. (He was the older brother of Judah Roberts, who replaced their father, Joel Roberts, after he was released for disability, on the Connecticut Line. Judah

Joel Roberts's gravestone. Roberts was another Revolutionary War soldier who left the service due to illness. His fifteen-year-old son, Judah, replaced him. *Author's photo collection.*

was just two weeks short of his fifteenth birthday when he joined in August 1778—they were the two youngest soldiers who enlisted from the town of Winchester.) In the Eighth Regiment, Roswell Catlin and Phineas Smith represented Winchester.[67]

October was a busy month for the military in 1777. Not only was Washington engaging Howe, but there were also feints by the British to raid the largest military supply depot in Fishkill, New York. The British did attack Peekskill again but did not go further. To ward off this threat, a contingent of men, all from Winchester, was sent to Fishkill and led by Ensign Peter Corbin of the Seventeenth Regiment, Seventh Company, on October 6. The men included Sergeant Jonathan Coe, Sergeant Eliphaz Alvord, Sergeant Robert McCune, Philip Priest, Joel Roberts, Darius Gibbs, Samuel Clark, Samuel McCune, Nathan Blackman, Daniel Andrews, Nathaniel Balcom, Samuel Preston and Ichabod Loomis. They returned at the end of October when the threat had passed.[68]

In the meantime, the Battle of Freeman's Farm in the first battle of the Saratoga Campaign had occurred on September 19, 1777. A badly outnumbered General John Burgoyne had managed to hold off the Americans in what was a stalemate. The final battle of Saratoga took place on October 7 at Bemis Heights. The numbers favored the Americans, twelve thousand to four thousand, but "Granny Gates," as Arnold called his superior and nemesis, refused to let the brilliant general fight. Angered at his loss of command, and possibly drinking heavily in his cabin, Arnold decided to ignore the command, as he saw the chance of victory slipping away. As he rode up to a group of militia, he hailed them and found that he had found a Connecticut militia, Colonel Lattimer's. They, and others in Poor's and Learned's Brigades, followed him to root out pockets of the British; several men from Winchester were in these units. As the British and Hessians were drifting back into the forest, Arnold rode his horse between two redoubts, and both he and his horse were hit by gunfire. Arnold won the day but almost lost his leg. It would be months before he could sit again and many more before he could walk. He would never command another American army.

Ten days later, Burgoyne's army was surrounded and surrendered to Gates. The prisoners of war, known as the "Convention Army," would first go to Boston. Most of the army went via New York to Massachusetts; some of the thousands of prisoners took a route what would later be known as the Boston Post Road through Connecticut, but a smaller group of 128 Hessians went via the "Green Woods." The Green Woods extended from New Hartford to Norfolk, including the Old North Road of Winchester.[69]

Upon arrival in Boston, the prisoners did not get to board a ship for Britain. The colonies wanted their upkeep and expenses paid by the British in gold, and they also insisted on Burgoyne providing a list of the prisoners' names in order to fulfill the terms of the surrender. Burgoyne resisted. He would eventually be sent back to Britain, but the soldiers were then marched off to Charlottesville, Virginia, at the behest of Thomas Jefferson in the latter half of 1778.

The seven-hundred-mile trek to Virginia included a not-so-leisurely stroll through the roads of Connecticut again, primarily led by militia to the border of New York. A large contingent, primarily of Hessians, again passed over the Green Woods road, led by General Poor. One left his account of this portion of the road:

> *November 22nd, 15 Miles.*
> *The march through the mountains, or the so-called "Green Woods" to Nortfolk* [sic] *which we took today, had been described to us something very bad, and we were expecting the worst road possible. However, our*

expectations and every idea of a very bad road were still surpassed. It was certainly hard work to take a brigade of four regiments with six cannon and a lot of baggage 14 miles through the woods, down a very steep mountain, then up again another one still higher and steeper, and so on. Sometimes rock of 3–4 feet circumference lay in the middle of the road. It was very cold, and the water coming down the mountains was frozen, which made the ascents and descents very difficult for men and almost impossible for horses. In short, everything was surpassed that could be called a bad road, since in addition the valleys were so swampy that it was almost impossible to walk through them.[70]

Meanwhile, many of the same men who had accompanied General Washington in the Battle of Germantown in October 1777 would enter their winter quarters at Valley Forge that December, including the men from Winchester, although three—William Leach, Phineas Smith and Samuel Roberts—were discharged in January.[71]

At Valley Forge, hunger was unavoidable. Washington was not used to carrying more than two days of rations with his army. The cold was unbearable for men who did not have sufficient clothing or shoes. Yet those who survived came out a fighting force. Starting in February 1778, Baron von Steuben became their drillmaster. An experienced Prussian soldier, Von Steuben wrote drills for the army, standardizing the methods, thereby coordinating the Continental army. In addition, Washington's aide-de-camp, the nineteen-year-old Marquis de Lafayette, helped with the drilling and improved morale and shared much of the suffering of the troops.

When the army emerged from winter quarters, it was a well-trained fighting unit. General Howe had resigned after his poor judgment in not supporting General Burgoyne, thus losing an entire army, and was replaced by Lieutenant General Henry Clinton. On June 28, 1778, Clinton was attacked at Monmouth, New Jersey, by Washington's army from the rear. The Connecticut men who had remained in Valley Forge in the spring were in the battle. On a fiercely hot day, the battle raged, and eventually the British withdrew back to the Monmouth Court House. As night fell, Washington set his men up in positions for the next day's battle. Clinton decided to forgo another battle and used the cover of darkness to retreat. As the British had planned, they retreated to New York City and left Philadelphia to the Americans.

The last important battle in the Northeast occurred less than a week after yet another raid by Governor Tryon in Connecticut in July 1779. The raid was a ploy to try to get Washington's troops to move into the open so that the British could fight a major battle and "end it all." Washington didn't budge, and Connecticut had to call out its alarm companies and militias. A few days later, Washington got his revenge.

The battle took place on July 16, 1779. Stony Point, located at the mouth of the western bank of the Hudson River, controlled passage to West Point. It was defended by redoubts of cannons fronted by abatis, whose sharpened points would keep troops at bay. In addition, the redoubts were set on a steep, rocky precipice, partially surrounded by the swampy riverbed, which during low tide was only two feet deep.

Rather than attack frontally, Washington and his field commander, Brigadier General "Mad" Anthony Wayne, decided on a stealth approach. They called in the Corps of Light Infantry, formed only one month earlier. This was the army's most seasoned and well-trained unit. Eight companies of Connecticut men were in the column of 150 that attacked from the south, the most difficult portion of the undertaking. Two were from Winchester: Daniel Potter and Jonathan Preston.

Undercover at night, with unloaded muskets, two of the three approaches were led by "Forlorn Hope" units of twenty men each attacking from the north and south. Meanwhile, the largest group of Continental soldiers attacked from the center with muskets blazing to divert attention away from the rocky climb made by the other two columns. The wade through the water—which unfortunately was four feet deep when they crossed— alerted the British. Nevertheless, under fire, the Forlorn Hope contingents were able to chop down the abatis to allow the remaining two columns of soldiers to attack with their bayonets, but not without heavy casualties. Casualties among the Forlorn Hope units were estimated at 90 percent. Within half an hour, the 564 British troops were captured, dead or injured. The Continentals had no intention of remaining at the fort; instead, they tore down the defenses, took the fifteen cannons, military supplies and anything of value and left.

The following year, Daniel Potter was promoted to corporal, but Jonathan Preston deserted, possibly because his wife was expecting what would be their only child. At a town meeting in Winchester on March 26, 1781, it was voted "Captain Corbin to make Application to procure a pardon for Jonathon Preston on account of his Deserting the Army." He had fought in five major battles.[72]

Soon the British moved back in but only stayed a few months. Other than another raid in 1781, a vicious attack on New London by a disenchanted

Benedict Arnold who had turned traitor, Connecticut remained relatively unscathed. The British army concentrated elsewhere. The real victory for the Americans was that Henry Clinton no longer wanted to be anywhere near the new professional American army—an army that now added a more covert, lethal guerrilla warfare to its repertoire. Once word was received that France had entered the war on the side of the Americans, Great Britain removed many troops from North America and sent them to the West Indies to guard their lucrative island possessions. The remaining British army in North America turned its attention to the southern colonies, where Loyalists and slaves might support the goal of separating New England from the South—this time by attacking the South.

In the last years of the war, thousands of Connecticut men still guarded the Hudson River Valley and the Connecticut borders, while others in the Continental line went south with Lafayette, playing hide-and-seek with the British troops under the command of various British officers like Phillips, Tarleton, Arnold and Cornwallis. Seth Stannard and Remembrance Filley were in the Light Infantry under Captain Welles's Company in the Third Regiment, Connecticut Line. They, under Lafayette, stormed the redoubts at Yorktown on the night of October 14 and were present when General Cornwallis surrendered on October 19, 1781.[73]

Although the British army in the South had been captured, many Continental troops remained on the Connecticut Line until the peace treaty was signed in Paris on September 3, 1783. This uneasy period of time between the successful engagement at Yorktown and the release of troops after the Treaty of Paris was recounted by the granddaughter of a courageous widow, Hannah Everett, who struggled to keep her family together in the wilds of Winchester during that period:

> *During the severe winters of that period, the hungry wolves howled in the little enclosure of my grand-mother's cottage during the nights, and were seen to jump over the fence when any one opened the door. Many are the incidents related in my childish ears, of the sufferings of the family during the revolutionary war, particularly in the "hard winter" of '83.*
>
> *No grinding could be done at the mill—snow fell every other day for six weeks—and the wind and drifting seemed only a continuation of the storm! Grain and corn were boiled for family use. Wood was drawn on the tops of the drifts, on a hand-sled by my Uncle Andrew (the youngest son) on snow shoes, and received by his sisters through a window at the back of the house. My Uncle Noble at this period was a chaplain in the army, and my father*

Hannah Everitt struggled to keep her family together during the Revolution. Her family recorded the details, and this became the basis of a short story by Rose Terry Cooke. *Author's photo collection.*

(Josiah), also away getting his profession, and afterwards in command of a company on the Canada frontier.

During the hard winter a piece of check-woolen for soldier's shirts was put into the loom, but it was impossible to weave it on account of the cold; so it was all wound out in balls, then doubled (one thread white and the other blue) and twisted on the "great wheel"; and thus prepared, my grand-mother and her four daughters sat in a circle, enclosed by blankets suspended from the joists overhead around the high fire-place—and knitted the yarn into stockings for the army. One night during these times, my grand-mother and her children sat up amid the howlings of the winter blasts, in consultation whether they should break up housekeeping and each take care of themselves. After retiring and passing the remaining night sleepless, grandmother arose in the morning, and told her family that "by the help of God they would keep together."[74]

Nevertheless, many residents of Winchester and all of Connecticut found the years following the Revolution extremely difficult and migrated north and west—a factor not caused by war but certainly aggravated by it.

Chapter 4

WINCHESTER AND THE "GREAT EXODUS"

The town of Winchester's population grew steadily, or so it seemed from the public records. In 1756, there were 24 residents; in 1774, just prior to hostilities, there were 339. Near the end of the war, in 1782, the population more than doubled to 688. By the turn of the century, the population more than doubled again to 1,371. However, by 1810, the increase was down to a trickle, only increasing to 1,466, just 95 more than the prior decade; by 1820, the population had increased only by 135 residents! The increased numbers barely suggested what was actually happening. The "Great Exodus" from Connecticut had caught up to Winchester.[75]

"All the towns of Litchfield County were seriously retarded in their growth by this first emigration westward, and not one of them so irretrievably as Old Winchester....Numerous old chimney places line the lonely roads where, in 1800, large families were reared and school houses crowded." John Boyd was partially correct. Roads made western lands more accessible. However, it was not the reason for leaving.[76]

Winchester was, at first, the recipient of settlers moving in from other towns in Connecticut from the midcentury until the middle of the Revolution. These settlers were escaping from their unwillingness to deviate from primitive agricultural methods. They worked the fields until the fields were played out, then they moved to greener pastures. Those greener pastures were actually the marginal western lands of Connecticut, which included Winchester.[77]

In addition, the original settlers refused to follow the British system of primogeniture, where the eldest son received the home and the land, while younger sons went into the ministry and the military. Colonial families in Connecticut divided up their land among all their sons—and families were large. In Barkhamsted and Colebrook, for example, both towns asked the state for abatement of their taxes in 1780 due to the poor yields of crops. They were having difficulty feeding their large families, which comprised "the younger part of life." Various sources indicate that the state was densely populated considering the status of its agricultural, home manufacturing, commercial mode of life. In other words, the population was too large to adequately feed and clothe its populace.[78]

Another contributing problem was Connecticut's economy during and after the Revolutionary War. Paper money issued by the Continental Congress and that issued by the state quickly devalued, whereby the phrase "not worth a Continental" joined the lexicon. Lack of hard specie hindered virtually all transactions near the end of the war. For example, Hannah Everitt's daughter, Diana, was invited to a wedding and desired a new dress. The intrepid Hannah rode miles away to the nearest store, "where she found a pattern of chintz, which she could have for eleven and a half yards of checked woolen shirting for soldier's wear; but could not buy it with continental bills." Diana, determined to have a new dress, "carded, spun, washed, and put into the dye-tub, one run of yarn, and so the work went on; the cloth was wove the 'gown pattern' purchased, made up, and worn to the wedding at the week's end." Unless one had gold, the economy, for many, had returned to bartering.[79]

Poor agricultural lands were the push—the pull was new lands opening after the war. The Oneidas and Tuscaroras were the only tribes to side with the Americans in the Revolutionary War. To honor them, the new U.S. government prohibited the buying or taking land from Indian nations without federal approval. Governor George Clinton of New York ignored this directive, which caused Oneida sachem Good Peter to claim, "He did not say, 'I buy your Country.' Nor did we say, 'We sell it.'" Nevertheless, the governor took it. Oneida County was open to settlement by 1788. It was the first choice of many migrating families, particularly from Litchfield County and the Berkshires.[80]

Thirty-eight families were listed on Baschard's Patent for the ownership of "an oblong square of six acres, now known as Vernon Center." A myth started that the reason for leaving Winchester was due to a vote in 1786 that placed a new church on the Green in Winchester Center rather than in the

Danbury Quarter sector: "The Danburyites became so disgusted with the whole proceeding, that they left their homes in a body (August 1797) and started westward to pastures new, traveling in wagons drawn by oxen. After consuming two weeks in the journey, bound to have a 'Center,' and a Green of their own, they founded Vernon Center, N.Y." That is neither the reason nor the timeframe.[81]

Seth Hills, Winchester's first deacon and first state representative in the town, went to Vernon, Oneida County, New York, in 1798 to clear acreage for his future home. This was an area "without a white inhabitant, save two or three who went with him." The following year, he brought his family, which included his stepson, Stephen Goodwin, to their new home, and the group included Abijah Peck Brownson, who had recently married Hewitt Hills's daughter, Mary. This followed a pattern—many men not from Winchester married women who were. They followed their fathers-in-laws at a later date to Vernon Center—some did not actually settle in that town but rather in Floyd, Westmoreland or Augusta (a large segment of the young men lived there in 1800 according to the census). Of the thirty-eight names, only nineteen families, including the sons-in-laws who were not from the area, can be considered from Winchester.

Thomas Spencer, a successful tanner and merchant who lived on Lake Street in Winsted (Spencer Street is named after him) and married another daughter of Hewitt Hills in 1795, owned a store with his father-in-law and moved to Vernon with Hewitt. Other men came to Winchester in the 1790s but left for the promised land of central Oneida County. Some in Winchester who left were only children at the time of the vote for the new church, like Matthew Griswold, who left for Vernon between 1802 and 1807. Half of the families listed on the patent were either not from Winchester or never left Winchester for Vernon Center. Levi Marshall from Torrington moved to Westmoreland, near Vernon, but his brothers Seth and Harvey never lived in New York, although they were listed on the patent. They spent most of their lives in Colebrook, Connecticut, although Seth died in Ohio.

Reverend Publius Booge is named in the patent. This seemed to give credence that the families were following the minister. He was not even in Winchester when the vote for the church occurred. He became the minister of the church five years after it was built. He asked to be dismissed in 1800 due to ill health. He did go to Vernon Center but did not become the preacher. He left in 1803 to become the minister of a church in Georgia, Vermont, returning to a town near Vernon Center in 1815 to preach until the preaching of evangelist Charles Grandison Finney drove him into retirement.[82]

Poverty was also not the reason for this particular move, as these were relatively wealthy farmers and businessmen from Litchfield County and the Berkshires who were listed on the patent and moved to Oneida County. The inducement may well have been the opening of the Genessee road, which ran from Albany, New York, to Pennsylvania, bringing more markets within reach. That the Greenwoods Turnpike, which ran from Hartford to Albany, was completed by 1800 made transportation much easier, as well as reflects John Boyd's analysis of the roads being an important factor in migration.[83]

Another locale also saw an influx of Winchester residents: Vermont. Eastern Vermont was dominated by Connecticut residents from central and eastern Connecticut. Not so western Vermont. Ethan Allen's brother, Ira, one of the Green Mountain Boys, had an "ingenious scheme" during the Revolution and for a short while after: no taxes on land. This was achieved by selling confiscated estates of Tories. Early residents included David Austin, a man of "advanced age" who in 1796 moved to Waterbury, Vermont, "induced by crafty misrepresentations to exchange his Winsted property… for wild lands in the State of Vermont which proved to be nearly worthless," according to John Boyd.[84]

The Allens (no friends to the Congregational Church) also attracted those who sought escape from religious restrictions. "Nineteen out of twenty-one Congregational churches organized in Vermont by 1780 were located east of the mountains." Whether this was the impetus for John Hills is unknown, but he moved to Charlotte, Vermont, in 1781, carving a homestead out of the wilderness in western Vermont.[85]

Remembrance Filley (spelled "Philley" once he removed to New York in 1800), more than most, may have had other reasons for leaving Winchester. His brother, William, from whom he inherited a portion of the land that had formerly belonged to Caleb Beach, died at a young age by drowning. Unfortunate incidents seemed to dog him.

Remembrance enlisted as a private throughout the war, ending his career at Yorktown. Meanwhile, his first wife may have filed for a divorce while he was off soldiering. He remarried in 1786. His first son had died at birth, although his second son survived. Upon arriving back from the war, he must have had huge debts, as soldiers had difficulty in collecting their pay and were given what amounted to promissory notes upon the close of the war. In 1782, a tax list revealed that former soldiers who had served only a portion of the war, like Joseph Hoskins, had thirty-nine pounds taxable property;

Captain Peter Corbin had fifty-six pounds taxable and Samuel Hurlbut ninety-three pounds. A black farmer, Eli Dolphin—whose son, Richard, probably served—had thirty-seven pounds, while Remembrance, who had served all eight years, had but one pound. His status was not much higher than "pauper."[86]

Filley remarried in 1783 and started a second family that soon grew to more children than he could afford. Between 1784 and 1792, his wife gave birth to four daughters. In 1791, the town used the "revolting system of bringing town paupers to the auction block." Boyd quoted the town record:

> *Voted, that the selectmen be directed to take charge of Remembrance Filley, and conduct with him as they shall think most for his comfort, and will be least expensive to the town, whilst he remains in his present state of delirium, either to set him up at vendue (auction or public sale under law) to the person who will keep him the cheapest, or dispose of him in any other way which may appear to the selectmen more convenient, and for such time as they may think reasonable, and on the cost of the town. Ensign Bronson bid off Remembrance Filley at eight shillings per week for two weeks, and at ten shillings for two weeks after. Samuel Wetmore second bid him off to keep him two weeks at ten shillings per week.*

Boyd then mentioned the sorry state of lunatic asylums, but this was actually not about lunatics—descendants think that he may have been delirious, perhaps due to a case of malaria that he might have contracted in Virginia during the war. Yet it does appear to be clearly a case of taking care of a destitute family for a few weeks, not some manic action.[87]

In 1800, Filley removed his growing family, which now numbered two young sons and three daughters, to Rensselaerville, New York. In 1807, he purchased one hundred acres of land in McDonough, Chenango County, New York. By 1818, he had six acres cleared and a log house and an even larger family. Before he died in 1837, his three sons—Isaac, Uriah and Elijah—all had farms. It is unclear where the idea came from that he died a pauper. This was the type of success story that migrants dreamed when they brought their families north and west of Connecticut.[88]

At the request of the state, a report on the status of Winchester and Winsted was written by the first town clerk of Winchester, Eliphaz Alvord, in 1813. He stated that "the emigrations from this society have been more numerous in years past than of late, they have been chiefly to the westward and northward and so irregular as to admit of no correct estimate." His report was complicated by the fact that a great many had moved into Winchester from other areas of Connecticut—that almost compensated for the massive emigration. By 1820, the pattern of growth would improve dramatically.[89]

The town would often lose residents in periods of economic distress or due to the introduction of a generous land policy. After the Civil War, for example, when farmers' sons would take advantage of the Homestead Act of 1861, Winchester would lose some veterans who now had the opportunity to go west and start a farm with little cost other than to get to their destination. Nevertheless, the population continued to grow because laborers and artisans would move into Winsted to work in the factories and become industrialists or merchants. But some people just could not stay in one place.

The parents of Eli Foster Lewis and his brother Isaac Ives Lewis moved from place to place within Connecticut. Eli was born in Winsted in 1820 and his brother in Meriden a few years later. The family moved to New York and then on to Illinois, where the boys' mother died. Eventually, the brothers and their families moved to Minnesota territory and then Wisconsin. The American government made a treaty with the Sioux Indians of Minnesota territory in 1853 to open the land to settlement. In 1857, Eli bought land from a half-Sioux Indian and founded Winsted, Minnesota, named after his birthplace in Connecticut. (He didn't stay there, as he eventually moved on to help his brother in a mining operation in Ketchum, Idaho, where Eli died in 1885.) After the Civil War, residents of Winchester could be found in most states and territories in westward (and even southward) directions; nevertheless, massive industrialization had grown to such an extent that Winsted, a village within the town of Winchester, had become the hub of commerce in northwest Connecticut.[90]

Chapter 5

THE EARLY REPUBLIC AND THE TOWN

AGRICULTURE AND MANUFACTURING

In the Winchester-Winsted status report of 1813, Eliphaz Alvord reported to the Connecticut Academy of Arts and Sciences on the status of agriculture and industry in the Winchester Society, while James Morris, Esquire, reported on the Winsted Society.

In response to questions asked, Alvord reported that the soil in Winchester was fifteen to eighteen inches deep, with hard gravel beneath. The best use of the land, he explained, was for grasses, which gave rise to livestock rather than crop production, though he was quick to point out that "with judicious cultivation it produces very good crops of various other kinds." The types of grains attempted were rye and oats, along with Indian corn, flax and grass. "The quantity of grain of any kind produced is generally not luxuriant, the soil not being so natural to grain as grass. Grass has yielded more than four tons an acre at one crop." He stated that "the quantity of land planted with potatoes, and sown with turnips is unknown perhaps 28 acres." He claimed there was no reason for rotation of crops since the main crop was grass. Unlike other areas of Connecticut and its agriculturalists, he stated that the best fertilizer was from "the stable," not plaster of Paris, which was recommended by late eighteenth-century scientists.[91]

As for livestock, Alvord reported a law that required the enumeration of sheep as of January 1801 in the various towns. The entire town of

Winchester had 1,599 sheep that were at least ten months of age. Alvord stated that there was no number available for swine and that the number of beef for market was difficult to ascertain because "a part being barreled here and part being driven alive into markets, and to different places."[92]

His agricultural report concluded that for other markets, little cider, maple sugar or garden crops were produced other than for household use. Butter for market was available for sale, but the quantity unknown. However, the quantity of cheese for other markets was considered to be not less than twenty-five thousand pounds annually.[93]

As far as manufacturing, in the Winchester Society, "many families manufacture the woolen clothes they wear in the family but very little for market." Further, "there are no furnaces or forges in this Society, nor mills of any description except sawmills, & one or two bark mills." Why? Because "there are no rivers or streams of any considerable importance, there is however a stream running through this society known by the West branch of the Waterbury river, on which stands one sawmill."[94]

Within the Winsted Society, Morris noted that there were two streams: the Mad River originated in Norfolk and emptied into a stream called the Still River. In the Winchester Society, the Little Pond emptied into the Long Pond (Highland Lake) in the Winsted Society, which "furnishes a great number of mill seats and important waterworks in Winsted."[95]

Alvord also described the two turnpike roads running through the town. In the Winchester Society, the Waterbury River Turnpike Road, passing through Winchester to New Haven, was not used as much as other roads, although it did allow for a tavern nearby. In Winsted, the Greenwoods Turnpike (now Main Street, not to be confused with the Green Woods Road, of which the Old North Road was a part), which had been recently built, was kept in good repair. He claimed that on this road there were two bridges, "neither of them remarkable for elegance."[96]

At the end of his portion of the report, Alvord described a common occurrence in the town of Winchester: "On the 31st day of January 1807, the Earth being then frozen to an uncommon depth; a storm of rain commenced, and increased so rapidly, that in a short time streams were swelled so that Mills & Bridges were swept off by the violence of the flood."[97]

James Morris described the economic activity of the Winsted Society as having five ironworks, mostly from working the pig iron brought from Salisbury, a distance of twenty-three miles. Six trip hammer shops made axes, scythes, sleigh shoes, drawing iron for wire and plating for gun barrels. Also mentioned were two gristmills, four sawmills, one carding machine, one clothiers works, one factory for cutting nails that employed twelve workmen and an establishment for making wooden clocks—"three thousand made in the past year." Also, there were three tanneries, which processed hides into leather, utilizing the wood most conducive to the process, hemlock, which Winsted had in abundance. And then there was card making. Child labor was used in setting the teeth in the cards used in the processing of wool fiber. Morris claimed that child labor "may prove an incentive to industry, at a period of life, when their hands cannot be usefully occupied in ordinary pursuits."[98]

One of the first major businesses was that of scythe manufacturing. (A scythe is an agricultural tool with a curved blade attached to a long pole for cutting grain or grasses.) Colonel Hugh Orr opened the first scythe manufacturing plant in Bridgewater, Massachusetts. Benjamin Jenkins learned the trade there and became the foreman of the second scythe manufacturer in the country, which was opened by Colonel Robert Boyd in New Windsor, New York, on the western bank of the Hudson River. Boyd's nephew, James Boyd, was an apprentice at the New York plant. James's sister, Elizabeth, married Benjamin Jenkins. Jenkins and the younger Boyd entered into a partnership after they became brothers-in-law. In 1792, they erected the third scythe establishment in the country along the Still River in Winsted. In 1802, they built another works on Lake Street after the building of the Greenwoods Turnpike made procuring supplies and access to distant markets easier and more profitable. The newly built Greenwoods Turnpike (1799–1800) proved a boon for entrepreneurship in Winsted, a mecca for manufacturers that required fast-moving streams to turn their waterwheels, which powered their factories and, with a turnpike, was a means to get the finished product to distant markets.[99]

Meanwhile, James Boyd wed Mary Munro, and the couple, with the Jenkins family, built an elegant home near the first factory on the Still River in 1795. As their families grew, the house proved rather small for two large families, and Boyd moved to a house near the Lake Street factory, which he owned after they dissolved their partnership. The Jenkins family moved into the tavern he built on the site of the current campus of Northwestern Connecticut Community College. This situated Jenkins near the Main and Rowley Street scythe factory he built in 1812 and which became the site of the former Strong Manufacturing Company and, most recently, was home to the Office of the Community Lawyer. The small mansion on the Still River eventually became the beloved home of the renowned author of the second half of the nineteenth century Rose Terry Cooke, and in the twentieth century it was removed to

Norfolk. An apprentice of Boyd and Jenkins, Merritt Bull, built another scythe shop on Meadow Street. By 1872, three large scythe manufacturers combined produced 250,000 scythes per year.[100]

Just a few years after Jenkins and Boyd opened their first scythe establishment, they partnered with Thomas Spencer Jr. to erect the first iron forge in Winsted, on Lake Street, using the power of the Lake Stream. The iron they refined would be utilized in the manufacturing of the scythes they produced, among other implements.[101]

The year 1799 brought the Rockwell brothers from Colebrook to Winsted to build their iron forge, completed in 1802, across from where the Solomon Rockwell house, now the Winchester Historical Society, is located. A forge was built on the Still River in 1811 by Reuben Cook and others.[102]

The iron and scythe businesses would dominate Winsted's early manufacturing, especially due to the complementary nature of the two business models.

Elias Balcom's saw- and gristmills were first taken over by Ensign Jesse Doolittle and later rebuilt after the Winsted flood of 1807 by Samuel and Luther Hoadley. The Hoadley brothers, originally from Waterbury, came to Winsted in 1803 and purchased land, a dam and water rights on the Still River; they erected a sawmill on one side of the river and a gristmill on the opposite side. After the flood, in addition to rebuilding the mills, they replaced the bridge, which had also been destroyed. At this point, they built a small shop on the east wing of the bridge, on the south side of the road, and began manufacturing wooden clocks. They also brought into the business their brother-in-law, Riley Whiting, who had married their sister, Urania.[103]

For a short while, the brothers also made bells and erected a factory to make wire, which was successful during the War of 1812. However, after the war ended, the business could not compete with foreign competition. Luther, appointed a captain during the war, died in Groton on September 8, 1813. His brother, a lieutenant colonel, survived the war and returned to Winsted to continue the business with his brother-in-law under the name of Hoadley & Whiting. Five years later, in 1819, Whiting bought out Samuel Hoadley and in 1827 purchased Luther's share from his widow.[104]

Riley Whiting manufactured shelf and pendulum clocks, all of whose gears were made of wood. He manufactured tall case clocks until about 1830. Some of his clocks were of the pillar and scroll design, but most were shelf clocks that had stenciled and carved cases. There is in existence one "wag-on-the-wall clock" made by Riley. Basically, this is the clock movement and face. This type of clock may have originally been intended to be a long case clock, which peddlers went door to door selling to customers with the belief that they would build the clock case themselves. It is only one of two clocks of this variety known to have survived.[105]

Riley Whiting died while on a business trip in 1835 and left the business to his wife, Urania. Their fifteen-year-old son, Riley Whiting Jr., continued to make the clocks until the estate was settled. In 1841, Urania Whiting sold the brick and the wooden clock shops, along with a sawmill and other pieces of land and machinery, to Lucius Clarke, William L. Gilbert and Ezra Baldwin for $5,000. The new owners formed a firm called Clarke, Gilbert & Company for the manufacture of brass clocks. Clarke and Baldwin would leave the concern, and in 1846, the William L. Gilbert & Company was formed and soon became the largest manufacturing concern in Winsted.[106]

Another major business that proved to be long-lived were tanneries. Colonel Hosea Hinsdale would move to Winsted in 1802. He had not planned to stay in Winsted, but the tanning properties of hemlock had recently been discovered. If Winsted had a town tree, the hemlock would definitely have been in the running since it was commonplace throughout the town. He built the tannery on the stretch of land that eventually became the front lawn of Shadow Lawn and is now the home of Dunkin' Donuts. Hinsdale and his brother-in-law and partner, James Shepard, would utilize the School House Brook, which at the time ran above ground instead of under the Mary P. Hinsdale School and was conducted through pipes into vats where the hides were kept. The power for grinding the bark and moving the paddles in the vats that kept the hides in motion was not through water power, but rather the primitive method of yoking a horse to a capstan in the grinding floor and having the horse roll the stone by walking in a circle, grinding the bark into fine particles as well as stirring the water in the vats. This, then, was the process for making leather to be used in making shoes.[107]

James Shepard dissolved their partnership in 1810, purchased land on West Main Street and built another tannery. This was purchased in 1832 by George Dudley, who had disposed of property in a tannery on the Greenwoods Turnpike, two miles east of Winsted. Upon commencing business in Winsted, Dudley decided to use sheepskin instead of cowhide for what became one of the most successful business in town throughout the nineteenth century as the market expanded to other products.[108]

The carding machine (which James Morris seemed to feel kept the idle hands of small children from the devil's work) was located in the Shepard and Miller Tannery (better known as the Loomis Tannery) in 1812. Another concern was set up by the Hoadley brothers in their gristmill. There were

Urania Hoadley Whiting's brothers were clockmakers. Her husband, Riley Whiting, purchased their business, and after his death, she sold the business to entrepreneurs, including William L. Gilbert. *Author's photo collection.*

two sets of machines, one used for cutting and bending teeth and another for pricking the leather (possibly why the location in a tannery). Of course, children had to insert the teeth into the leather but worked from home under the guidance of their parents. Another machine would fasten the handles to the cards.[109]

The carding shops started manufacturing at the beginning of the War of 1812 and ended shortly after the war was over, both because of cheaper cards from England and because newer machinery was invented to combine all operations. This was, however, an important step, along with the fulling operations and the clothier shops, as wool would need to be passed through the carding operation—the resulting yarn, when woven, would need to be cleaned and thickened and made into cloth. These businesses would have fits and starts in the early decades of the nineteenth century, but Americans did overtake the British by the end of the century and two very successful businesses in Winsted were the result.[110]

But in the decades after the war, not only was manufacturing begun, but the communities in the Winchester Society and the Winsted Society were also being enlarged.

CHURCHES AND THE GREENS

Soon after its incorporation by the state assembly in 1768, the Ecclesiastical Society in Winchester voted that the Sabbath meeting be held until December 1769 at the John Hills house, which was near or on the current Hurlbut Cemetery on the South Road. The society then started work erecting the first meetinghouse, where the members worshiped for the next seventeen years.[111]

The first meetinghouse was primitive in construction, seating was rough planks or slabs; as membership grew, loose boards were laid over the overhead crossbeams. Access was gained by a plank ladder outside. A "Sabba day" house was built nearby in which a large fireplace was used to warm parishioners between the morning and afternoon services, as there was no heat in the meetinghouse other than "foot stoves," which required coal for heating.[112]

Eventually, a new meetinghouse was required, and in 1785, Dr. Josiah Everitt, the son of Hannah Everitt, deeded to the First Ecclesiastical Society land for a house of worship and "a suitable green around the same." The vote on acceptance was close: the Winchester Center members winning out by six votes over the Danbury Quarter members.[113]

The Green was used not only by the church but also by the authorities to punish those whose behavior was deemed unacceptable, as well as by the militia, who were expected to train, especially in the era between the Revolution and the War of 1812. The church stood in the center of the

Isaac Bronson's sketch of the house he built, probably around 1800. He died in 1849, leaving the property to his son, Theron. *Connecticut Historical Society*.

plot. On the Green across from the tavern was the whipping post, and to the south of the Green were the stocks. Both were painful and publicly humiliating to whatever poor miscreant ran afoul of the rules. The militia training of 1793 was described by a descendant of Colonel Ozias Brownson (Bronson), who commanded the regiment. "Tables were set in Dr. Everett's orchard, where the Bronson homestead now stands. The ladies came arrayed in silks, satins, damasks, and changeable lutestrings, of all colors….Standing together, across the road from the Green, near General Hurlbut's, out of range of the enthusiasm of some luckless soldier's gun, they added a picture of color, and beauty, to the scene." He continued: "After the training exercises, good old fashioned baseball was played upon the Green….Wrestling, foot races, leaping, and pulling on the rope were practiced."[114]

The meetinghouse remained on the Green until the third meetinghouse was built in 1841 on land leased from Isaac Bronson, whose view was blocked by the church on the Green. It was stipulated that "nothing should ever be erected again in front of his house."[115]

If the Ecclesiastical Society of Winchester seemed at times to be acrimonious, the Ecclesiastical Society of Winsted outdid it. For thirteen years, the residents of the eastern sector of Winsted and the western sector of Barkhamsted argued about the placement of the church. They pitched a stake, time and again, on the proposed site, but the stake refused to stay stuck! Finally, the meetinghouse was erected in Winsted, but near the Barkhamsted line in 1793. However, that was not the end of the story. Once the Greenwoods Turnpike opened in 1799, the meetinghouse followed as more and more inhabitants moved into Winsted. East Street bisected what is now the Green. The church was located on the western side of the road facing east. It would remain there until the church was moved off the Green, a little farther to the west in 1848 at what is now the entrance to the parking lot of Northwest Community Bank.[116]

The Green in Winsted was also the site of many of the annual musters of the Twenty-First Regiment. The regiment consisted of four companies, with the plumes in their hats and, in some cases, their uniforms differentiating the towns. Winsted had black plumes; New Hartford wore white ones, as did Barkhamsted, which also wore blue coats and white trousers; and Riverton wore "showy uniforms, plus a nodding plume of red and black."[117]

SCHOOLS

As was typical in New England villages, the First Society of Winchester, Connecticut, first established a church and then in 1773 voted "two pence on the pound" to support a school. Through the next few years, the taxable rate was increased, and by 1778, there were five districts in the First Society (Winchester). Probably most classrooms were in the homes or barns of inhabitants, although there were those who reminisced about the "Two Chimney Schoolhouse" probably located on the site where the Little Red Schoolhouse (District 8) now stands near Winchester Center.[118]

Connecticut's General Assembly ordered towns to organize into educational societies. The sale of Connecticut's western lands in Ohio were expected to compensate the societies for educational costs. However, the expected funds did not materialize due to the occupation of the British army, which had not relinquished its forts after the American Revolution in the Western Reserve and Canada. The British allied themselves with the Native American inhabitants, who successfully held back settlement of the area for decades. Therefore, by the early 1800s, in the First Society of Winchester and the Second Society of Winchester (Winsted), the expense of the school was borne by those whose children attended within the district the family lived. Taxation was assessed by the number of chimneys a homeowner had in his house. Apparently, each fireplace in a home was assessed a tax of $1.25 annually to pay for education.[119]

In 1796, it was voted that the Second Society (Winsted) would have seven districts. The subsequent growth of Winsted in the first half of the nineteenth century encouraged the growth of school districts. The size, shape and number of districts fluctuated yearly until 1843, when the number of districts increased to a record high of fourteen, while the First Society (Winchester) maintained its five districts, creating a total of nineteen districts.[120]

Private schools and academies flourished in Winchester and Winsted for those students whose parents saw the need for education beyond the "no frills" education of the early public schools As mentioned before, the method of taxing for education was via the number of fireplaces. This had the wealthier and more progressive parents, who saw the value of education beyond what was offered in the districts, at a disadvantage. In 1810, in the village of Winsted, there were four homeowners taxed at the $5.00 rate, eighteen at $3.75, sixty-four at $2.50 and sixty-nine at $1.25. The less affluent families determined the level of education, and for many of them, education beyond primary school and the rudimentary "three Rs" held no value.[121]

Private schools during the century were paid by parents depending on how often their student attended. Some students were to provide their own seating, and all textbooks were the responsibility of the students (as were textbooks in the public schools until the middle of the twentieth century). Some schools survived decades and others for only a few years.[122]

Although by 1799 the Greenwoods Turnpike for the first time united east Winsted with west Winsted, the isolation of the two had already set in. For more than a century, bickering between the two sections occurred, unless, of course, they turned their attention to "the Flats" the portion of Main Street in the center of town that was reviled by both sections. Lending libraries through subscription or tax were established in both sections, and the argument over the post office required a post office in both villages. In 1833, the West Village petitioned the General Assembly to establish the borough of Clifton, ostensibly to tax those residents for a fire department. However, conservatives were elected to the board, and there was little will to encourage taxation. Per usual, they wanted the fire department but not the tax; therefore, the borough languished until absorbed by the establishment of the borough of Winsted in 1857.[123]

Chapter 6

LEADING FAMILIES OF WINCHESTER, 1800–1870

Hurlbut

When Samuel Hurlbut and his brother-in-arms, Ozias Brownson, journeyed with George Washington across the Delaware, these two men little knew that they would become the fathers of the two leading families in Winchester.

Captain Samuel Hurlbut began, as so many did, as carpenter, joiner and farmer. He then operated a tavern in Winchester Center decades before liquor became anathema in the town. As a farmer, he quickly realized that land in Winchester was best suited for grasses and the livestock that fed on them. In his later years, he engaged with his two youngest sons in "country trade." In addition, he was the town's choice as a representative for seventeen terms in the General Assembly.[124]

John Boyd quoted Reverend Frederick Marsh, the pastor of the Winchester Center Congregational Church, when describing the life of Captain Hurlbut:

> *He closed a useful life, after having lived in the parish fifty-nine years, and enjoyed a good share of respect and confidence as a magistrate, and in other departments of public business. Having been one of the earliest inhabitants, and having purchased a large quantity of land in the center*

of the parish, he did much to promote the settlement of the place, by disposing of his lands on so easy terms as to induce others to settle here. The public green and ground, on which the meeting house stood…were given to the Society by him.[125]

Of the four sons who survived to manhood, Silas, his eldest, died at the age of twenty-four. His second son, Leonard, became a large dairy farmer, with his residence about a mile northeast of Winchester Center. One of his contributions to horticulture was the Hurlbut apple, "the finest kind for November and December," according to the *Hartford Daily Courant* in its "The Farm and The Garden" column. The third surviving son, Samuel, received his name not only from his father but also as a reminder of the son who died at the age of eighteen months. Samuel and Lemuel, the youngest sons, are those best remembered for their "country trade" in the largest store in Litchfield County and for Lemuel's outstanding accomplishments as an agriculturalist, with special emphasis on animal husbandry.[126]

The S. & L. Hurlbut store, with its gilt-lettered sign, was situated where the Grange and post office building would be located after the brothers' deaths. Samuel never married and was uncomfortable in social settings. Described as a "capable, thorough, careful business man, he managed the affairs of the firm in its various business with skill and great ability, accumulating an estate perhaps the largest ever known in the place." He was also the postmaster. He was perhaps not as outgoing as his affable brother Lemuel, yet one person remembered the "gusto" with which Samuel read aloud from the *Connecticut Courant* this vignette:

"Which of these is the road to the village of Winsted?" Asked a traveler of a barefooted urchin whom he saw near a fork in the road. "Either of 'em it don't make no difference which" replied the boy, "but which is the best one?" "Ain't nary one of 'em the best, take which you are a mind 'ter and before you get half way you'll wish you'd took t'other one!"[127]

Lemuel was not a behind-the-counter type like his brother Samuel. This genial man was an acknowledged agriculturalist and successful breeder of livestock. Early on, he reduced the rocky, hilly terrain of his land to "smooth and fertile fields." Chief among Hurlbut's cultivation was the addition of root crops, particularly carrots. Unlike the emerging belief that grain and grasses should be fed to cattle, he added root crops to the mix for their winter feed, with excellent success.[128]

Sheep, horses and cattle at different periods received his skill in animal husbandry. In 1812, he obtained some Merino sheep. He continuously added to the flock, with the able help of a shepherd, continuing to breed them as purebloods until 1824, when he began a cross-breeding program with what were then called Saxonies to produce "some of the best fine-wool sheep ever introduced into the United States." He sold his sheep in 1840, disposing of many thousands over the years with prices ranging as high as $200 per head. Between 1818 and 1830, he raised horses as well as sheep, but his most outstanding accomplishments were with cattle.[129]

In 1817, he was given a gift of six North Devon heifers and a bull from a British peer. Two years later, he purchased more cattle from the same source:

> *He spared no pains or expense in improving his stock of beef cattle, that could also be used as oxen. For the rest of his life he was engaged in this business and sold over fifteen hundred head of Devons. Cattle from his herd were purchased throughout the states and became a staple in the beef industry. The unrivaled strings of pure red working oxen that grace the agricultural fairs of this county, attest to valuable service he performed for the agricultural interest of this region.[130]*

This was not Lemuel's only job. The firm of S. & L. Hurlbut was a large dealer in cheese, selling from 200,000 to 500,000 pounds annually, and Lemuel was the salesman of the product. He introduced improvements to the product, thereby increasing the company's profits and enabling the store to pay its farmers a very reasonable price—in cash, if they chose. The product found its way to markets in New York, Boston and Baltimore, a city he visited 170 times. The finest hotels, like the Astor House, among others, offered cheese from S. & L. Hurlbut to its guests.[131]

Neither Hurlbut, after the nationwide Panic of 1819, bought goods on credit. Yet if a neighbor fell into temporary hard times, the Hurlbuts acted as bankers, charging no rate higher than 6 percent. They also lent money to farmers who wanted to add to their farms and stock. In Winsted, if a resident had good security but wanted to borrow money, Samuel would lend it to them, since the nearest bank was in Litchfield until the Winsted Bank opened in 1848. In 1854, a second bank was planned; the presidency was offered to Samuel, but he declined the position. He did, however, purchase a large amount of stock and paid for engraving the first plates of the notes, which bore the likeness of the two brothers. As a way of thanking the brothers, the bank was named the "Hurlbut Bank." It opened in 1857.[132]

After Lemuel's death in 1856, Samuel's health, physical and mental, rapidly declined, and he died the next year. No one stepped forward to purchase the store, and the business dissolved. They were buried in the orchard of their farm, now known as the Hurlbut Cemetery on the old South Road, just a little west of the South Road cemetery.

Brownson/Bronson

Colonel Ozias Brownson (with later generations changing the spelling to Bronson) was a blacksmith and had a farm south of Winchester Center. Bronson and his wife, Abigail Peck, had one daughter and six sons, the last son, Isaac, being the only one born in Winchester. Descriptions of Ozias include the words *fierce, overbearing, industrious* and *thrifty*. His sons carried forward many of his attributes.[133]

His namesake, Ozias Bronson Jr., could apparently build anything—"a house, a cart, or a plough, or any other article of wood and iron." He built a home for his family in Winchester Center on Chapel Street but sold it to Reverend Frederick Marsh in 1802 when he left for Amsterdam, New York. Levi Bronson owned a large farm near the southeast corner of Norfolk, where he lived with his wife and their ten children. The description of the third son, Salmon, included the terms *industrious, frugal, honest, moral* and *steadfast*. The apple on the Bronson tree never seemed to stray far from the path of their father. Asahel Bronson was a successful farmer like the rest of his family and shared many of the same industrious characteristics. His house on Blue Street, where he lived and died, is still standing. He married rather late in life, wedding Lophelia Richardson on July 26, 1824, and died less than three months later. Abijah Bronson was rather more adventurous than his brothers. After he married Hewitt Hills's daughter, Mary, they moved to Vernon Center, New York, with many members of the Hills family; there, he did not, according to John Boyd, accrue land or fortune as successfully as did his brothers. Isaac also married a Hills daughter, Eliza, but remained in the town where he was born. He built the house that he and subsequent members of his family lived in and inherited. He was a farmer, a merchant and the largest landowner in Winchester Center. Of his eleven children, six were daughters; of his five sons, several died young and others moved away, so his business devolved on his sixth child, Theron, who would also inherit the homestead.[134]

Above: The Isaac Bronson House is located near the Old Waterbury Turnpike and the Congregational Church and across from the town Green in Winchester Center. *Author's photo collection.*

Right: All of Isaac Bronson's sons were great builders and carpenters. Many of their homes are still standing, including the Asahel Bronson House, located on Blue Street. *Author's postcard collection.*

As did most farmers in the area, Isaac specialized in dairy. Isaac and Theron worked closely together, owning several farms not far from the Green and controlling others. They often had cattle drives through town to change pastures or to drive newly purchased cows home. They would run businesses and invest in others that would bring them larger markets. That didn't make them very popular with one family in town, the Hurlbuts. Isaac opened Bronson Supply Company, a store near their home on the north side of the town Green that competed with the S. & L. Hurlbut store nearby. They sold not only supplies and lumber but also dairy products, as Isaac had at least fifty milking cows. It so enraged Lemuel Hurlbut that he proceeded to build his magnificent Federalist house across from the Winchester Green on the south side—but facing away from the Bronson's store in protest. Nevertheless, Isaac was popular with much of the town of Winchester, as he was elected a justice of the peace and three times a representative in the General Assembly.[135]

After Isaac died in 1849, Theron ran and increased the family business with a cheese box factory and a sawmill and invested in other ventures that supported his and the community's interests. Theron encouraged and partnered with Gail Borden to open a plant in Winsted on Willow Street in the midst of the Civil War, where the recipe for Borden's condensed milk was perfected. The plant was in operation from 1863 to 1866, utilizing milk from the numerous dairies in the town and beyond. The building still stands.[136]

Theron invested not only in Gail Borden's venture but also in other businesses, including the Connecticut Western Railroad, which expanded options in getting farmers' produce and dairy products to wider markets, as well as lumber, a business his children would expand. He also invested in the future of his children and others by becoming an influential contributor to the Winchester Institute, a boarding and day school founded by Reverend Ira Pettibone and, coincidentally, located not far from his residence.[137]

Theron also found time to serve as a representative in the General Assembly (1849) and as selectman in the same year. He also served many years as justice of the peace (1842–64). In 1871, two years before his death, he served as chairman of the town's centennial celebration. After his death, his sons Edward, Wilbur and Elliott carried on and expanded their father's businesses into the twentieth century, opening another store in Winsted.[138]

MARSH/CARRINGTON

Winchester Center could boast of a family whose members were known not for their skills in agriculture or business acumen but for their piety. As a descendant, Judge George Carrington explained in notes for a speech he would deliver: "There was a company of people in Winchester in the '40s and '50s that in intelligence, dignity and worth constituted a good specimen of a typical New England community. They were industrious in their business, kind and social in their dispositions, well informed in their minds, feared God, sustained public worship, provided education for their children, served well their day and generation." Carrington claimed that "stability" in the ministry was the reason for such an outcome.[139]

He gave credit to the thirty-seven-year active ministry of Reverend Frederick Marsh, his grandfather, who served from 1809 to 1846 in the Congregational church at Winchester Center, as well as those who served after him, including the fifty-year ministry of Reverend Arthur Goodenough, who also wrote about Reverend Frederick Marsh in his book, *The Clergy of Litchfield County*.[140]

Frederick Marsh, born in New Hartford in 1780, studied with area clergy before attending Yale in 1805. He preached in Winchester in 1808, but when the Ecclesiastical Society met in November that year and voted thirty-three to one to offer Marsh the position of pastor, he refused due to the lack of unanimity and because he could not afford to purchase a house without going into debt. In December, they voted again, and he received a unanimous vote total of forty-two, with no opposition. He resided in the house built by Ozias Bronson Jr. on Chapel Street.[141]

As a pastor, Marsh believed in the "eternal and unchangeable truth of God." He took life seriously and frowned on frivolity. Other pastors found that "his influence over his brethren was silent, modest, not obtrusive; not so much that of great intellectual power as of sincerity, truth, self-sacrifice and unfeigned devotion." "Modest, cautious and painfully conscientious" he struggled with some of his beliefs, particularly regarding the death of children in early infancy and their future in the afterlife. He suffered "deep melancholy" over the possibility of their fate even after the question was discussed by a ministers club to which he belonged in 1814 and whose members agreed that some of the children who died in infancy were likely saved.[142]

Marsh's suffering extended to the possible fate, both in this world and the next, of his own son, Jonathan Pitkin Marsh, a deaf-mute child. Fortunately,

Judge George Carrington was an insurance agent and judge of probate. He was also one of the first members of the board of directors of the Memorial Library. *Connecticut Historical Society.*

Reverend Thomas H. Gallaudet, who knew Frederick Marsh from Yale, visited with the family in Winchester Center. Gallaudet had established the American Asylum for the Deaf and Dumb in Hartford in 1817. After Gallaudet watched little Jonathan's attempts to communicate with him, he told Mrs. Marsh, "Your son tells me that you keep a horse, two cows and many sheep." An amazed Mrs. Marsh wept tears of joy since this was the first time anyone had been able to communicate with her son. Jonathan was sent to Gallaudet's asylum, where he met and eventually (in 1840) married Paulina Bowditch, also a deaf-mute.[143]

Reverend Frederick Marsh married Parnal Merrill in 1809, and they had seven children, including a set of twins. Two of the daughters died in childhood or early adulthood, but their daughter Catherine married Reverend George Carrington, with whom she had two sons, George and Edward, and a daughter, Louise. She returned after her husband's death to live near her husband's parents in Colebrook with her eldest son, George, while her two youngest lived with her parents on Chapel Street in Winchester Center.

It is Catherine's son, Judge George Carrington, who wrote so lovingly of the Winchester Center Congregational Church around which his grandfather had so much input in shaping:

> *For notwithstanding the faults and imperfections of its membership which are fully and freely conceded, the church is the bulwark of righteousness in the community. It is the nucleus around which good influences rally, the pillar that can be leaned upon to support all helpful causes, the finger to the moral eye that, like its tower to the natural eye, always points upward.*[144]

Chapter 7

THE LEADING FAMILY OF WINSTED, 1800–1870

A tragedy in nearby Colebrook led to the emergence of the preeminent family in Winsted: the Rockwells. Needing a stream of fast-running water to run their iron forge, rather than the pond whose befouled waters were blamed for the illness and death of some Colebrook residents, four of the Rockwell brothers—Reuben, Solomon, Alpha and Martin—purchased the water rights of David Austin in 1799. They moved one of their forges to Winsted in 1802 onto the Lake Stream, which had previously fed Austin's mills.[145]

The purchase of the former Austin property from the current owner, John Sweet, included more than one hundred acres of land, several houses and barns, the sawmills and the gristmill, as well as the water rights from Long Pond (Highland Lake). This did not include the water rights accorded to the Jenkins and Boyd scythe operation, which was dissolved a few years later with James Boyd retaining ownership. Solomon and Alpha moved to Winsted to take charge of the operations of the business. Solomon moved into one of the houses that came with the Austin property. Alpha, who married in 1800, built a house on the corner of Main and Lake Streets that, years later, would be removed to build the Beardsley House.[146]

Promptly after moving to Winsted, Solomon, at the age of thirty-five, decided it was time to marry and chose Sarah McEwen, the daughter of a

The Solomon Rockwell House, built in 1813, was also known as "Solomon's Temple" for its grandeur and because it overlooked many of his properties along Lake Street. *Author's photo collection.*

prominent family from Winchester. They married on July 2, 1800. Sarah was a decade younger but had experienced a great deal of heartbreak when it came to choosing a husband. Years earlier, she had broken off with a younger man just hours before their wedding, most likely at her parents' insistence. Many years later, as an elderly woman, she would read in a newspaper that her first love had died impoverished and drunk. Solomon, however, proved to be an excellent husband and father. When Sarah mentioned that she would like to live closer to Winsted, her husband commissioned "Solomon's Temple" on the corner of Rockwell and Lake Streets, a magnificent mansion that was the work of Captain William Swift, an architect from Colebrook, and was completed in 1813. The mansion portrayed Rockwell's eminence as not only a businessman but also a town leader. He served a term as a representative in the state's General Assembly and fifteen years as the town's justice of the peace.[147]

Solomon and Sarah's only child, Jerusha, was born in 1803. She attended Winchester Academy and later was sent to boarding school in Hartford. This insistence on education for a daughter was a relatively new idea. Prior to the American Revolution, it was feared that education was unhealthy for the supposed feeble brain of women. But the rationale for "Republican Motherhood" was that women had to be educated in order to teach their

The stairway and hall of the Solomon Rockwell House as it looked when Mary P. Hinsdale lived there. The Winchester Historical Society purchased the house in 1920. *Connecticut Historical Society*.

young sons. Jerusha would follow suit with the education of her daughter and stepdaughter.[148]

In 1822, Jerusha, along with her father, traveled by stage and then by boat on Lake Erie to Cleveland to view some of his many properties in Connecticut's Western Reserve, located in a 120-mile strip of northeastern Ohio. This monthlong journey may have included the town of Austinburg, named after one of his partners, Eliphalet Austin of Norwalk, who brought families from Connecticut to reside there in the early 1790s. Rockwell also had many properties in Lenox, Ashtabula County, as well as properties in Astabula Township, Knox and Rutt. His properties in Cuyahoga County included Bedford, Chagrine and, most importantly, Cleveland. Sales of land in the Connecticut Western Reserve to speculators like the Rockwell brothers put money into a fund for public education in Connecticut.[149]

Prior to Rockwell's death, he deeded more than three hundred acres in Cleveland to the Western Reserve College, which during Rockwell's lifetime was located in Hudson, Ohio, moving to Cleveland much later in the century. He also set up an endowment fund for the school. When his generous gifts are considered, one might gather that Rockwell approved of the college's abolitionist sentiment, which was particularly strong during the 1820s and '30s, when the school was one of the most important centers of the antislavery movement.[150]

A few years after Jerusha's trip, she wed her neighbor Theodore Hinsdale. Hinsdale's father, Bissell Hinsdale, had purchased property on the opposite corner of Lake and Main Streets from Alpha Rockwell in 1800. There Hinsdale operated his mercantile business. His primary business was selling cattle to be slaughtered and sold in the West Indies. He also purchased cheese from the area farmers to be sold out of state.[151]

The same year, Hinsdale's son, Theodore, was born. He attended Yale University, graduating in 1821. Living just down the hill from the Rockwells thrust him into the circle around Jerusha, and they wed in 1826. Theodore moved into the Rockwell home. Two years earlier, S. & M. Rockwell obtained the scythe shop on Meadow Street on the Lake stream from the estate of Merritt Bull, who had been an apprentice to Jenkins and Boyd. After Hinsdale's marriage, Theodore joined the family business, and the business adopted a new name, Rockwell-Hinsdale.[152]

In 1837, Hinsdale, a member of the state legislature, brought forth a plan for the Connecticut Joint Stock Act of 1837. Up to this time, every shareholder was held liable for all the debts of the corporation. This act, which was quickly passed, held shareholders liable only for the value of the stock held. His father, Bissell Hinsdale, had been a victim of the prior law when he had cosigned papers on his brothers' business, which failed. The debtor's law at that time involved imprisonment. He was put under house arrest for two years. Undoubtedly, the passage of this law encouraged investment in new businesses in Connecticut and eventually throughout the country.[153]

Jerusha and Theodore had three children: Sarah, born in 1827; Mary Pitkin, born in 1828; and Solomon Rockwell Hinsdale, born in 1835, two years after the six-year-old Sarah died of scarlet fever. Several tragedies in addition to the death of the young Sarah befell the Rockwell-Hinsdale alliance in rapid order: in 1837, Sarah Rockwell died at the age of sixty-two; Solomon Rockwell died at the age of seventy-four in 1838, possibly following a heart attack; and in 1841, Theodore Hinsdale died of typhoid fever, leaving Jerusha bereft. In her diary, she recorded:

> *Theodore Hinsdale, my dear husband, died of Typhoid fever November 27, 1841. May I be able to say, "thy will be done." I have strength and wisdom to bring to my two children. Mary was (13) two weeks before her father's death. Solomon was (6) years the August before. Oh, be a God to the widow and a father to the fatherless.*[154]

Two years after Hinsdale's death, Jerusha married the widower John Boyd. John was the son of James Boyd, who along with Benjamin Jenkins had started the scythe business in Winsted. John knew Hinsdale not only from living in the same town but also from attending Yale at the same time. They also studied law in the law office of Seth Staples and his partner, Samuel Hitchcock. This law office would eventually be absorbed by Yale Law School.[155]

John's twin brother, James, went into business with his father but died in 1826; therefore, John came back to Winsted and took his brother's place in the business. He married Emily Beers in 1831 and had three children, one of whom died when a toddler. Emily died a few months after their third child was born in 1842.[156]

John Boyd moved into Jerusha's home with his two daughters, Ellen and Emily, joining the Hinsdale family of daughter Mary and son Solomon. Little Emily, always sickly, died in 1852. Jerusha's daughter, Mary, like her mother, was sent to a private school in Hartford and following graduation attended the prestigious Mrs. Willard's school in Troy, New York. Ellen Boyd received her additional education at the Ipswich Female Seminary in

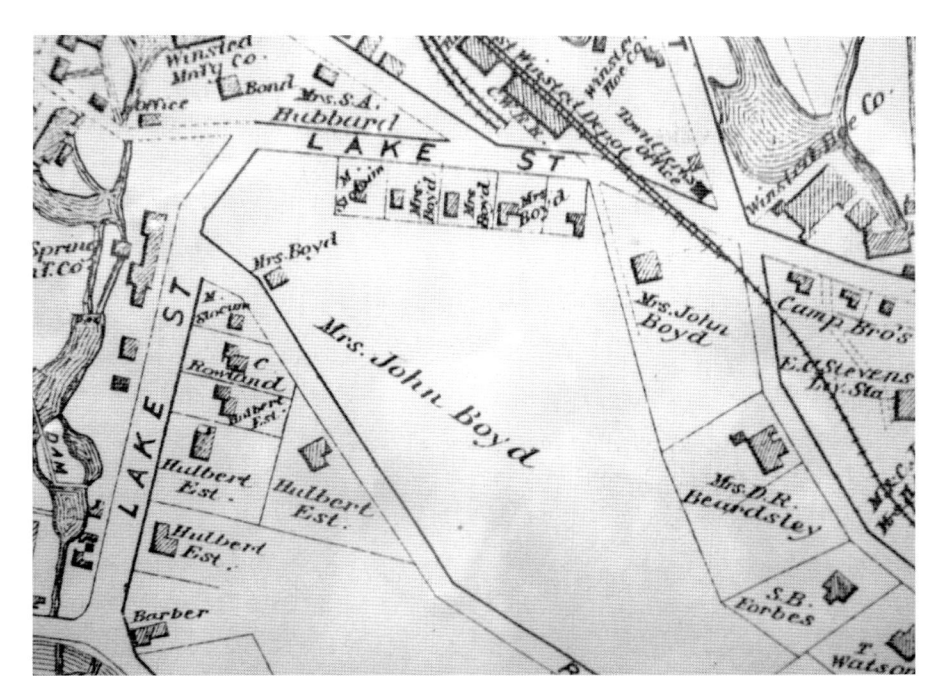

The Lake Street portion of the 1874 DeBeers map that shows the extent of the property owned by Mrs. John Boyd (Jerusha Rockwell Hinsdale Boyd). *Beardsley Library*.

New York. Jerusha's son, Solomon, was active in the Civil War, serving as assistant paymaster in the U.S. Navy, after which he served on the Mississippi Flotilla above Vicksburg until prostrated by fever and compelled to resign by impaired health. Eventually, he returned to Winsted and became the first conductor on the Connecticut Western Railroad.[157]

John, in addition to his responsibilities to his family's business, began a political career. He was town clerk of Winchester for thirty-three years, served as judge of probate for fifteen and served as a county commissioner. On the state level, he served as a representative in the General Assembly, one term as state senator and three terms as secretary of the State of Connecticut. He was also Winchester's first historian, completing a 633-page volume in 1873, *The Annals and Family Records of Winchester, Conn.* Jerusha Hinsdale Boyd died on March 11, 1875, and John Boyd died on December 1, 1881.[158]

Prior to Hinsdale's death, Theodore had taken on a new partner, Elliot Beardsley. Beardsley, married to Delia Rockwell, daughter of the late Alpha Rockwell, had been taken on as partner due to his business acumen. The scythe factory was renamed Hinsdale-Beardsley. After Hinsdale's death,

Elliot Beardsley owned the scythe factory outright, with the name changing to Elliot Beardsley and then to the Beardsley Scythe Company in 1851. In 1853, Beardsley, aware that the local iron forge industry was being replaced by imported, higher-quality steel from Norway, sold the upper forge while retaining the scythe company.[159]

Beardsley saw the need for a hotel near his Lake Street businesses. On the plot of land where his father-in-law's house had been located on the corner of Lake and Main Streets, Beardsley erected the elegant Beardsley House in 1848. The Winsted Bank, chartered the same year, moved into the Beardsley House, as Beardsley was one of the directors of the new bank. Two years later, the Beardsley & Alvord mercantile business relocated to the Beardsley House. In 1856, the Eagle Works cutlery business, which made pocket knives sold at Beardsley & Alvord, closed its doors. Still envisioning a booming market for cutlery, Elliot Beardsley and James Alvord built a factory on the Lake stream and began making cutlery in a very successful business known as the Empire Knife Company.[160]

Beardsley served in the General Assembly as a state representative and as a senator. He also served as a selectman in town for several terms that coincided with the village of Winsted, in its entirety, being chartered as a borough, which made the western side of town's charter of the borough of Clifton moot.[161]

When Elliot Beardsley died in 1871, he was remembered as being "reticent and deliberate by nature and habit, he minded his own business entirely, yet had an eye on all that was going on around him, and participated influentially, though quietly in public affairs. No man in the town was more looked to for advising and giving a direction to all measures for public interest; and patriotism." His wife, Delia, honored him in 1874 by donating $10,000 to start a subscription library located in the Beardsley Block, located next to their hotel, in a room built expressly for that purpose.[162]

The first librarian appointed was Miss Louise Carrington, who served for thirty-seven years in that capacity of head librarian. She was the granddaughter of Reverend Frederick Marsh, one of the leading families of Winchester, now working for a member of a leading family of Winsted toward the goal of educating and serving the public.[163]

Chapter 8

POLITICS, THE *MOUNTAIN COUNTY HERALD* AND THE ANTISLAVERY MOVEMENT

POLITICS

Political parties in the town of Winchester evolved quickly, though unevenly. Most businessmen were Federalists and then became Whigs after the collapse of the original party, while some of the surrounding farming community were Democratic-Republicans. The election of selectmen in 1797 did include some of the Democratic persuasion, although the Federalist Party quickly regained control the next year. The naming of a flood "of unprecedented magnitude" in 1801 the Jefferson Flood, which destroyed most bridges in the region requiring an extra tax of five mills on the dollar in town, was probably not meant to be complimentary to the new president of the United States.[164]

Philemon Kirkum, Esquire, moved to Winsted in 1800, and until he removed to Ohio in 1814, he was a Jeffersonian at heart—the sole representative of the Democratic Party in the village. Kirkum and some of his Democratic backers from the surrounding hill farms decided that a Democratic store should counter the Federalist store of Bissell Hinsdale. However, the Federalists would not allow him to build the store on Main Street in West Winsted. Nevertheless, he persisted. He built a store in West Winsted and, for good measure, one in the eastern village where his Democratic friends could purchase goods and discuss political principles. Unfortunately, farmers had much less money to spend than their Federalist counterparts, and the businesses had to close. In 1814, he moved to the Western Reserve and continued his political life in the Democratic Party, although he found unacceptable the views of Southern Democrats in regards to slavery.[165]

Political activism did divide the community during the War of 1812. Interestingly, in this second war with the British, the two parties reversed themselves in their time-honored argument of federalism versus states' rights. The Democrats during this conflict were the party of nationalism— "the state flag was then the supreme object of Federal worship." In 1814, the village Green in the eastern portion of town was the scene of some degree of violence, as "it took some minutes to detach the democratic fingers from the federal throat" when a newly erected Liberty Pole flying the national flag appeared to be an affront to a parade of newly recruited state troops, along with cavalry and an infantry unit arriving for their training day exercises. The flag was ordered down, but Democrats stood in the way. A Democrat grabbed the throat of the axeman, but a nearby fence filled with seated spectators came crashing down, disrupting the maneuvers; the militia was "marched off without the honors of war, and the star-spangled banner continued to wave until sunset."[166]

Physical restraint was not the only means utilized to keep Federalists from tearing down Liberty Poles during the war. A small field cannon purchased from Litchfield, a relic of either the French and Indian War or the Revolutionary War, was brought into service to protect the symbol of the nation. At a later period, it was used in an attempt to break up meetings of abolitionists, according to one historian.[167]

Mountain County Herald/Winsted Herald

During the 1840s, another political celebration—and the resulting percussive noise in the town that was surrounded by echoing hills— emboldened some women living in a hotel at the East Village who decided that they had suffered enough. After being within range of the booming cannon for half the night, they slipped out, and when the cannon was unguarded, they rolled the cannon into a garden and buried it. About a decade later, it was exhumed from its grave and did alternating service at political victories until the Republicans buried it again, hoping to resurrect it for what they believed would be a Republican victory in

1856. Unfortunately, the Democrats recovered it in time for the election, which Buchanan won. The victors punished the *Mountain County Herald*, a Republican newspaper, by blowing out its windows.[168]

The *Mountain County Herald* was the second newspaper in Winsted. The first was started by George B. Cooke, who began the *Winsted Advertiser* in February 1853. The goal was to secure fire protection, which the Borough of Clifton, in the western sector of Winsted, was supposed to but never accomplished. Cooke's editorial, in his first and only issue, stated:

> *Wanted, by the property holders of West Winsted, a sufficient amount of enlightened public spirit to induce them to provide the necessary apparatus for extinguishing fires. At present the whole apparatus of the kind owned in the place is supposed to consist of a super-annuated Squirt Gun, a tin horn and the "Winsted Fire Annihilator." The last of which, after soaking for one year in the dock at Bridgeport, and drying for another in the Greenwoods Turnpike, has at last been turned out to grass.*[169]

Ironically, the printing office owned by Mr. Cooke was destroyed by fire before the next issue was published. All that Cooke was able to save were a few fonts of type, but Thomas M. Clarke, twenty-three-year-old son of manufacturer Lucius Clarke and Nancy Boyd Clarke (sister of John Boyd), purchased all that remained of the *Advertiser* and hired Cooke as his printer. Clarke and partners Edward C. Stedman and Stephen Hubbard formed the *Mountain County Herald* in May 1853.[170]

The newspaper had not grown out of its infancy when, in January 1854, Clarke resigned and was employed by the *Bridgeport Gazette*. Soon Edmund C. Stedman became restless as editor, finding Winsted Society stultifying:

> *The great fault with Winsted people is that they don't know anything but money and financiering. There is not a man in town under 50 years of age, well educated in any other than a business line. They know how to make money, though. I am sometimes down in the blues for the lack of someone to talk to.*[171]

Although Stedman decided to remain in Winsted, he resigned his position as editor and entered into a new venture in which he would be joined by Hubbard. They founded the Winsted Coffee and Spice Company, whose brand of ground coffee was called Mad River Mills Coffee. The office was located directly across Main Street from the office of the newspaper. The business of roasting the coffee was carried on at Boyd's Machine Shop, and in March 1857, the coffee over-roasted and caught the shop ablaze. Soon after, Stedman left for New York and during the war became a journalist for the *Tribune* and the *World*. Afterward, he became a "money-grubbing" wizard on Wall Street as well as a famous poet.[172]

Meanwhile, upon the resignation of Stedman in 1855, Thomas Clarke returned to Winsted and took up the reins of the newspaper, which he then ran alone for a decade. He moved his office from the corner of Elm and Main to a new building that his father erected a little farther down on Main from the Winsted Coffee and Spice Company. His militant Republicanism brought on the cannon attack on this new building after the election of Buchanan. Nevertheless, the move was well-timed since, three months later, the office over the store that had formerly housed the *Mountain County Herald* was totally destroyed by fire.[173]

Strong in his opinions, Clarke's antislavery rhetoric found fertile ground in the town of Winchester, which, according to Parker Pillsbury, an agent of the Underground Railroad, was unusual for much of Connecticut. Pillsbury paid a visit to Winsted in the early 1850s and recalled:

> *After two weeks of wandering over a desert of pro-slavery indifference and hostility, a spot such as Winsted is a real oasis, a "Delectable Mountains" resting place to an anti-slavery agent. Almost everywhere, there will be one family to give me a good and welcome home; but beyond that, in Connecticut, we need not look for sympathy and support, except in very few and rare instances.*
>
> *In Winsted, there is a little band of chosen spirits. Their love of God is manifested not by reverencing holy days, holy houses, or holy ministers, but by acts of benevolence and humanity to his suffering children. They are hard laboring mechanics, eating none but the bread of patient industry; and they are a noble example of what working men and women can and ought to be.*[174]

This "little band of chosen spirits" evolved from a courageous group from Litchfield County that formed an antislavery society in January 1837, only fifteen months after William Lloyd Garrison, publisher of the antislavery journal *The Liberator*, was dragged by rope by a proslavery mob in Boston, intent on tar and feathering him, if not worse.

The Litchfield County men and women met in a barn in Wolcottville, since neither pulpit nor private halls allowed them a place to meet. Threats and rumors were levied against the band; nevertheless, the convention drew a full complement of hardy souls who braved the bitter cold and the rumors of retribution.

Reverend Daniel Coe of Winsted offered a prayer prior to the remarks of the guest speaker from the American Anti-Slavery Society. Roger S. Mills of New Hartford was chosen president, and among the other officers, Uriel Tuttle of Torringford and Jonathan Coe of Winsted were vice-presidents.[175]

While "counseling together for the relief of the oppressed and the elevation of humanity," a drunken mob gathered around the barn shouting imprecations, blowing horns and ringing a nearby fire bell; it later broke up the meeting by brute force. The convention was immediately offered use of the Torringford church, and there the members reconvened, deliberating for two days, emboldened in their defiance of the unruly mob they faced in Wolcottville.[176]

The Litchfield County Anti-Slavery Society held monthly meetings in various towns, meeting in houses, barns and groves while fulfilling its objective to raise the consciousness of the public with tracts, books and newspapers, much of which was printed by the Connecticut Anti-Slavery Society, whose antislavery newspaper, the *Charter Oak*, was printed from 1838 until slavery was completely outlawed in Connecticut in 1848.[177]

One of the very important (but, by necessity, secretive) activities by a small number of these activists was becoming an "agent" in the Underground Railroad, "where the panting fugitive was fed, clothed and speeded on his journey." Fugitive slaves' goal fleeing through northwestern Connecticut was to escape into New York State or Massachusetts at least until the 1850 Fugitive Slave Law made it necessary to "follow the North Star to Canada." This route on what is now Route 183 through Torringford was the most direct route to get to Winsted.[178]

Uriel Tuttle and Isaiah Tuttle both had "stations" on the Torringford road, both still standing. Uriel became president of the Connecticut Anti-Slavery Society until his death. From there, slaves perhaps went to Winsted, where they were entrusted into the safety of the town's own small antislavery society, chief among them being, undoubtedly, Jonathan Coe. Coe's station was located on Coe Street, where, according to his brother, Daniel Coe, slaves found sanctuary in a garret room until they either went to Colebrook and from there Massachusetts or west to Norfolk and on to New York.[179]

In Winchester Center, Noble J. Everitt was known to the secretary of the town's antislavery society. He was the grandson of the intrepid pioneer Hannah Everitt and may have opened up his home to runaways on the

Newfield Road. It is also believed that Silas Hurlbut McAlpine, who stood "in the front ranks of the despised little band of Abolitionists," probably kept fugitives as well, not far from Everitt's home on the Newfield Road. He was a schoolmaster at the chapel, as well as a poet, philosopher and owner of a cheese box factory in Winchester.[180]

One important resident of Winsted, the Honorable William S. Holabird, who in 1834 was appointed by President Andrew Jackson as a U.S. attorney for the district of Connecticut, was not amused by abolitionists. In 1839, he became the prosecuting attorney in the *Amistad* case.

Holabird considered the case to be that of murder and mutiny of slaves. He had no wish to try the case in court but wanted to turn the ship, its passengers and cargo over to the Spanish via diplomatic channels. However, Secretary of State John Forsyth decided that President Martin Van Buren could not interfere with the judiciary, thus the case went to trial with Holabird as the prosecutor. The defense attorney, Roger Baldwin, was able to prove that the mutineers had been kidnapped from Africa and were not slaves. Just as Holabird feared in a letter to Forsyth at the beginning of the trial, he stated that if the outcome were not as he and the administration desired, "I should regret extremely if the rascally blacks should fall into the hands of the Abolitionists, with whom Hartford is filled." The abolitionists had a field day with this case, organizing and collecting money for the prisoners and their cause. Holabird did not win the case, and it went to the Supreme Court, which ruled in favor of the Africans.[181]

A few years later, Holabird did win election to two terms as lieutenant governor of Connecticut but failed in his attempt to win the governorship to Roger Baldwin, the defense attorney in the *Amistad* case. In 1853, he penned a letter to another Democratic politician, warning him about the Litchfield Hills—apparently the propensity for that county was to vote Republican. When he died in May 1855, his obituary in the *Hartford Courant*, a Republican newspaper, made only a cursory announcement of his passing.[182]

On October 28, 1859, twenty-nine-year-old Thomas M. Clarke wrote an editorial in the *Winsted Herald* (formerly the *Mountain County Herald*) that broke with the policy of many abolitionists, who believed that moral suasion or political victory were the route to emancipation of the slaves. His homage to John Brown, the abolitionist born in nearby Torrington, not only poured his vitriol on the southern slaveholders and their government but also and especially on Republican newspapers that had formerly lionized the old man.

William S. Holabird overcame the onus as the losing prosecutor in the *Amistad* case to win election as lieutenant governor of Connecticut. *Connecticut Historical Society*.

In "Old Brown," Clarke began his tale with an explanation of why Brown chose to take over the arsenal at Harper's Ferry:

> *In an unfortunate hour (if it be unfortunate to suffer in a good cause), old Brown followed his stalwart sons to Kansas. There he soon saw two of them murdered under every circumstance of aggravated atrocity the mind can conceive, by the ruffian bands which sustained and countenanced by the reigning party and power in the national government, sought to force slavery upon the territory…he could no longer live if 'twere but for himself, and so consecrated his remaining energies to cheat the slaveholder of his prey and give "deliverance to the captive."*

He wrote that the Virginia governor who illegally tried Brown for a federal offense "gorges his soul with sweet anticipation of the sweeter tortures to be visited upon the old man, and the wholesome lesson he will hold up in the eyes of all 'Abolitionists,' and vows never to surrender him to the government above him."

Aware that the gallows lay in store for Brown, Clarke saved his harshest condemnation for Republican newspapers, politicians and Brown's prominent funders who went into hiding seeking to distance themselves from Brown:

> *And we may as well say, we have no admiration for that class of Republican newspapers which are so eager to disclaim and distance all fellowship and sympathy for old John Brown. Did they stop here, we could be patient with them; but when they go further and pelt him with the titles of madman, crazy muddled and insane, we cry out upon them for hypocrites and traitors, "little villains," unworthy to lick or feel the foot of old John Brown.…At all events he is unsuccessful, and so Republican presses the country over, fearful that their party will somehow lose a vote and themselves in office, fall to mouthing old Brown as heartily as twelve month since they praised, and vie with each other in denunciation and abusing him. For shame! Old Brown had more nobleness in his soul, more honesty in his heart, more principle in his action, more courage in a single finger, than all such politicians from Maine to Oregon.…He failed; had he succeeded, fifty coming years would have sanctified his grave with the holiness of a second Mount Vernon.… Alas, it was not so to be—the slave toils on in an unloosened chain, the hero gasps in a dungeon, and the Republican press cannot find room enough for their renunciations and denunciations of demented old John Brown.*

Clarke made a prediction:

> *For one, we confess we love him—we honor him, we applaud him. He is honest in his principles, courageous in their defense....Do with him as we will, his ashes will be written with the...Washington's* [sic] *of history, and the American school-boy shall yet be taught to listen with moistening eye and beating heart to the story of Old John Brown.*[183]

Chapter 9

"THE HEAVENS ARE HUNG WITH BLACK"

Winchester and the Civil War

Volunteers! Volunteers!
The Room over the Police Office, in Woodford's Block, is now open, and Col.
A.G. Kellogg will be present every day and evening to receive the names of all
patriotic citizens who are willing to enlist in a Volunteer Company—and hold
themselves in readiness to respond to the call of the Government.
Patriots, Come Forth[184]

Telegraphed messages from South Carolina on April 14, 1861, electrified the North as word about the attack and capture of Fort Sumter by Rebels was received before the Sunday morning church services. At least three churches in the town of Winchester notified their congregants of a meeting that evening at Camp's Hall.

Camp's Hall was the largest meeting hall in the town, and it was packed with worried citizens who drafted a letter to Connecticut governor William Buckingham asking that Connecticut "proffer its aid to the General Government in defense of the Union."[185]

Shortly thereafter, President Abraham Lincoln called for the enlistment of seventy-five thousand volunteers. The fiery newspaper editor of the *Winsted Herald*, Thomas M. Clarke, called for and presided over a meeting held again at Camp's Hall to encourage young men to answer the call for ninety-day volunteers to serve in the Union army. Clarke offered five dollars for the first man to volunteer. A slight, Irish-born teenager named Samuel

Samuel B. Horne, an Irish-born immigrant, earned the Medal of Honor, was selected as the ambassador to the Virgin Islands and later became secretary of labor for Connecticut. *Beardsley family files.*

Belton Horne stepped forward and into the annals of Winsted history. He was almost rejected due to his lack of weight, only ninety-five pounds. Yet due to his athletic ability and his pluck, the doctor reversed his decision. Little did anyone suspect what this youth, a graduate of the town's common schools and possibly a private school, would accomplish during the war and in his lifetime.[186]

Seven or eight more men joined at that meeting. It is uncertain when Caleb Newman, the bailiff of the town, passed around an enlistment form gathering more names from town. Recruitment from Winsted then spread into other nearby towns, which made enough men to form a company. Horne mustered into the Second Connecticut Volunteer Infantry (CVI) as a private in Company K, which, confusingly, is noted as State Organization Company B.[187]

Within days of the first company being formed, another company was filled with men from Winchester. One of the recruits, Charles E. Palmer, the twenty-two-year-old son of a West Winsted wagonmaker, was chosen to be a second lieutenant in Company F. His parents, Bennett and Marilla (Eggleston) Palmer, probably had mixed emotions regarding his enlistment—pride at his patriotism but dismay as they realized that their only remaining son would face untold dangers. They had already lost their other two sons. Anson, at the age of twenty-five, had succumbed to pleurisy while farming in the Nebraska territory in 1857, and Oscar, while teaching in Winsted, contracted a virulent strain of measles in 1860 and died at the age of twenty-four. What would be the fate of their youngest and only remaining son?[188]

Charles, a printer by trade, had worked from the age of seventeen to twenty at the *Winsted Herald* and left for a better job in that field in New York City. However, by 1861, he was back in Winsted, possibly to help his parents in their grief. His former employer, the *Winsted Herald*, described Charles as "a young man of superior intelligence, of the kindest and most winning manners, of inflexible integrity and unquestioned bravery," and the young man did not forget the newspaper when his country called. Throughout his career in the military, he wrote letters to the weekly newspaper describing military life. Palmer enlisted as a second lieutenant in the Second CVI, Company F, known as the Rifle Company E.[189]

Company K marched to the Willow Street depot of the Naugatuck Railroad for the trip to the New Haven camp on April 22 accompanied by martial music, banners and a crowd of well-wishers with tear-stained faces. They arrived in New Haven and were escorted to a hall near the depot and provided with a mattress and blanket. However, uniforms were not ready. Company B would be the last company in the regiment to receive its uniforms and equipment prior to its mustering in on May 7.[190]

The townsfolk, realizing that the need for uniforms was dire, immediately purchased materials. Tailors cut and supervised the making of uniforms, while women brought their sewing machines to Camp's Hall and, in a week of constant work, made up fifty uniforms, while women from adjoining towns provided thirty-three. More than one hundred woolen shirts were made as well.[191]

When Company F boarded for New Haven on April 25, the men's uniforms were ready. Thousands followed this company to the depot, and speeches were made by ministers of the various churches. The turnout was even more spectacular than what the company had sent a few days earlier, presumably since nearly all of the men were from the town. Half the men were mechanics, 25 percent were farmers and the balance were clerks and laborers.[192]

James M. Burton, who had only lived in town for a few weeks, enlisted in Company F of the Second Connecticut Volunteers and became the first Connecticut death in the war. He succumbed to disease at the United States Hospital in New Haven on May 10, only three days after mustering into the army. His funeral in Winsted was a grand affair, with Reverend Hiram Eddy of the Second Congregational Church officiating, and since little was known about this newcomer to town, the emphasis of the sermon was a fiery diatribe against the South.[193]

Charles Palmer's report of May 6, 1861, to the *Winsted Herald* described the sea journey of Company F to Fortress Monroe:

> *Today being Sunday, the Episcopal service and the Articles of War are to be read on the quarter-deck at 11 A.M....Orders are to allow of no boisterous mirth or singing other than sacred hymns. There seems to be no disposition to violate these instructions, as those that are not sea-sick are in that state of lassitude which care for nothing save to be let alone.*

A few days later, he wrote of an incident that shocked the men as they made their way up the Potomac:

> *We saw the first secession colors this afternoon. A schooner passed close to us, and was hailed with the usual demand to show her colors. The captain at first seemed thunderstruck, but collecting his wits soon, he seized a small Negro boy and held him up kicking at arm's length above his head with the remark "those are our colors." No attempt was made to shoot down either the traitor or his flag.*

BULL RUN

Daily life included constant drilling, particularly those skills needed in skirmishing, which became the role the regiment played at First Bull Run. One of the most difficult parts for the new recruits to learn were the bugle calls, which were to denote different positions. Therefore, an officer devised a much easier system using popular songs, which Palmer listed with the signals that the troops were to obey: "Advance—Yankee Doodle; Retreat—Pop goes the weasel; Rally on Battalion—Dixie; Double Quick—Dan Tucker…etc."[194]

Palmer also wrote about the capture of Colonel Abram G. Kellogg prior to Bull Run; he walked a pair of lovely sisters home, only to be captured by waiting secessionists when he arrived. And after the Battle of Bull Run—when the regiment was the first on the field in its position as skirmishers and the last off the field to try and hold off the opposing army—he reported that several Winsted men had been captured, though, fortunately, none killed.[195]

One of the men captured was Reverend Hiram Eddy. In June 1861, Eddy's fiery pro-Union sermons to his Winsted congregation brought him to the attention of Governor William Buckingham. Eddy was granted a leave from his pastoral duties at the Second Congregational Church in Winsted to become chaplain of the Second CVI at the behest of the governor, a position that was to last two months. The two-month leave stretched to more than a year, as the fiasco known as Bull Run (July 21, 1861) led to Eddy's capture by the secessionists.[196]

Eddy's capture was a nightmare for him and difficult for the Confederate army, which had no idea what to do with the prisoners. Thus began the constant shuffling of prisoners among the Southern prisons. Eddy was housed in five different prisons, some more than once. He began his imprisonment at the Tobacco Warehouse in Richmond, Virginia, later called Libby Prison, where he was held on two separate occasions. From there he sojourned to Charleston Prison in South Carolina, where he was held before and after his imprisonment in Castle Pinckney in Charleston Harbor. From Charleston, he was incarcerated in Columbia Prison and then back at Libby Prison. From there it was a short trip away to a nearby pork warehouse and former slave pen transformed into a prison in Richmond; finally, the best of the lot was Salisbury Prison in North Carolina, from where he was eventually paroled on July 26, 1862. By that time, he had lost so much weight his wedding ring fell off and his full head of black hair had turned white.[197]

Compared to Reverend Eddy, Captain Abram Kellogg's captivity, which lasted from June 22 until January 21, 1862, was relatively short. Others were not so lucky. Company K private James C. McCauley was captured after the battle and was paroled by the secessionists in May 1862, and Company F's Samuel A. Cooper accidentally delivered a message to Virginians during the battle since uniforms in this battle were not regulated. He knew that he had made a terrible mistake as soon as they spoke, but by then it was too late. He was paroled on June 2, 1862.[198]

For another private from that company, James G. Woodruff, his thrilling escape from capture was recounted in the August 2 edition of the *Winsted Herald*:

> *An instance of cool courage occurred in our (Co. F). James Woodruff on our retreat dropped out of the ranks at Vienna, and lay down at the foot of a tree for a little rest, thinking to regain his company in the morning. He had not lain long, before a party of the enemy came up and made him prisoner. They took away his rifle and left two of their number to guard him, while the remainder of the company went on after more captives. One of the guard after a time left, charging the other to take good care "that the d----d Yankee did not get away." Jimmy had a pistol under his haversack which in disarming him was not discovered, and watching his opportunity he sent a ball whistling through the skull of his captor and made the best of his way on to Falls Church.*

After Bull Run, the regiment's ninety-day enlistment was over. Not to be deterred, Palmer, upon reaching Winsted, immediately began recruiting another company that became Company E of the Seventh Connecticut Volunteer Infantry. Palmer was chosen captain. His letters to his hometown newspaper continued, giving the homefront a bird's-eye view of the experiences that he and his company endured.

Fort Pulaski

On March 14, 1862, the *Winsted Herald* published Palmer's most striking report, written on February 23 about the late-night preparations for the Siege of Fort Pulaski. He described the building of batteries located at Jones Island, a triangular marsh between the Savannah, Mud and Wright Rivers surrounding the "indestructible" Fort Pulaski built under the guidance of engineer Robert E. Lee in 1831. Troops had to unload cannons and equipment onto the island at night, without lights, while men and cannons were sinking into the ooze. He reported, not without a sense of humor that was always present:

> *The mud would not bear their weight without sinking them to the axle… in no place was the sticky mud less than knee-deep, and many a shoe was left at the distance of from two to three feet below the surface, the owner esteeming himself lucky if he escaped without his pants being pulled off in his floundering.*

He was less than enchanted with the flora and fauna of the Georgia coast and wrote this tongue-in-cheek observation:

> *It is much the worse place in which I ever saw troops quartered…a rank growth of bulrushes, and swamp sedge…of native animals the chief are alligators…then the ground is covered with a species of crab…there are mosquitoes by the million.…The Mr. Jones, after whom the island was named, must have felt himself a highly honored Jones by the compliment.*

On April 18, 1862, the *Winsted Herald* gleefully reported the fall of Pulaski and the role the Seventh CVI played:

> *We have no particulars beyond the scanty dispatches of rebel papers, but it is certain that the bombardment lasted but a day or two. They state that the pointed balls from our Parrott guns went entirely through the solid walls of the fort (six feet thick), while the bursting shell rendered the working of the guns an utter impossibility. The Conn. 7th regiment had the sole management of our batteries on the occasion. To Capt. Charles Palmer was entrusted Battery Grant—8 mortars of 17,000 pounds each. That all carried themselves gallantly there is no question.*

The late Charles Palmer was the choice of members of the Winsted GAR when they named their post the Charles Palmer Post No. 33. *Author's photo collection.*

Soon the Connecticut regiment was moved out of the fort to James Island, South Carolina. However, this next battle was a disaster. An officer left temporarily in charge decided—against orders—to attack at James Island, South Carolina, on June 16 without his superior's permission. To cross swampy terrain while charging a fort proved an impossible task. In addition, the fetid coastal environment, as Palmer surmised, caused more deaths than rifle or cannon—including, sadly, his own.

Typhoid fever did not keep Palmer from participating in the Battle of James Island, and the letter home informing Palmer's parents of his untimely death at the age of twenty-three on July 7, 1862, from Brigadier General Alfred H. Terry read:

> *At the time of the action on James Island he was so ill that, under ordinary circumstances, he would not have been in command of his company; but prompted by the devotion to duty, which always distinguished him, he led his company to the field, and gave to it and the regiment a splendid example of courage and firmness under most trying circumstances. The noble purity and uprightness of his nature and his eminently soldierly qualities had*

endeared him to us all, and had led us to look forward to a brilliant future for him; and we mourn his loss, not only as ours and yours, but as a loss to the country which he served so faithfully.[199]

The *Winsted Herald*, in its July 18, 1862 edition, eulogized the youngest Palmer:

It will be thought no disparagement or disrespect to others, we are sure, when we say that the loss of no one of all our numerous friends gone forth to battle could have occasioned a more general and deeper sorrow.

ANTIETAM

September 17, 1862. The bloodiest single day battle in American history—22,717 men killed, wounded or captured. One unidentified son from the town of Winchester wrote home that the exhausted men lay down the evening after the battle and woke up realizing that they were lying on dead soldiers. His father said that his son worried that "he might never be the same again."[200]

The town had a number of soldiers in Companies D and E in the Eleventh Connecticut Volunteer Infantry, as well as a few individuals in the other participating Connecticut regiments, particularly the Sixteenth. The Eleventh was tasked with capturing and crossing the bridge, now known as Burnside Bridge, at Antietam Creek. Georgia troops, however, had the high ground on cliffs surrounding the creek, protected by heavy foliage—450 Georgians raked the skirmishers with gunfire from these heights. A general charge of the Union army eventually dislodged the Rebels from the heights and the stone wall. The Eleventh assisted without ammunition, using bayonets. It lost 181 men, including every field officer, for that day's work. The Sixteenth Connecticut Volunteer Infantry fought in the bloody nightmare of the Cornfield, losing a great number of its recent recruits.[201]

Winsted and Winchester lost four men killed, with others wounded. The Eleventh CVI, Company D, lost Private Lewis Dayton of Winchester. Company E lost First Sergeant Hiram Roberts and Private William F. Coggswell. The Sixteenth CVI, Company G, lost Elliott Fleming.[202]

Interestingly, William F. Coggswell was a rare recruit. He was born in Barkhamsted in 1836. He married Clarinda Seeley of New Hartford in 1859.

The 1860 census found them living on her father's farm in Torrington, but by 1861, they were living in Winsted. In November of that year, Coggswell, a Black man, enlisted in the Eleventh CVI, Company E, a White regiment. He died in the action at Antietam—shot in the head. Clarinda, successfully petitioning for a widow's pension, moved back to her family's farm in Torrington, not returning to Winsted until 1896, dying there in 1905.[203]

A Black man in a White regiment was an extremely rare occurrence. Coggswell died in the battle that enabled President Abraham Lincoln to announce the preliminary Emancipation Proclamation freeing slaves—the Proclamation itself going into effect on January 1, 1863, if the secessionist states did not give up their arms. It would be another year before recruitment of Black soldiers in Connecticut was begun in earnest, although by then some of Winchester and Winsted's Black soldiers had already gone to Rhode Island to enlist.

PORT HUDSON

On the night of March 14–15, 1863, Admiral Farragut passed the Rebel batteries at Port Hudson, Louisiana, with his flagship, the *Hartford*, along with the *Albatross*, the only two that were able to get through the deadly fire of the well-placed Rebel batteries. At the curve in the river, Fort Hudson loomed impregnable on an eighty-foot bluff, well above the range of the ships under Farragut's command. However, with the two ships passing through the firestorm to the other side, the Red River and the Upper Mississippi were closed off to Rebel traffic, leaving Fort Hudson vulnerable to siege.

General Nathaniel P. Banks was a man with a mission. His poor showing in the Shenandoah Valley against Stonewall Jackson had been an embarrassment. His orders were to defeat Port Hudson, thereby allowing the Union army access to the entire Mississippi River, and then to rush to Vicksburg to help General Ulysses S. Grant's troops. He needed to burnish his poor military record in the East by winning big in the west, which, he felt would increase his political chances of winning the presidency—a goal shared by many other generals. Instead of allowing the siege to work, he tried several poorly thought-out attacks that set him back.[204]

The assault of June 14, 1863, was a terrible defeat for the Union. Five Connecticut regiments played a big role in this battle, and the Twelfth entered the ditch leading up to the parapet, where the assault was to be made before daybreak. The Thirteenth and Twenty-Forth were already at the ditch—their duty was to carry thirty-pound gunny bags of cotton to bridge the moats and to advance the charge. The Twenty-Sixth was in line of battle, ready to charge, while the Twenty-Eighth (whose Company F was made up of men from Winsted) had one hundred men assigned to hand grenade duty.[205]

Mark Wheeler had recently moved to Winsted with his second wife, Adaline Beach of Harwinton. Wheeler enlisted in the Twenty-Eighth Connecticut Volunteer Infantry, a nine-month regiment, and ended up at the Siege of Port Hudson. He was one of the one hundred men chosen as grenadiers to assault the heavily defended fort, many from the Twenty-Eighth. Mark Wheeler, in a letter written to his wife, wrote:

> *Today, June 12th, 72 men are detailed from our regiment who are to act as support to the 4th Wisconsin and 8th New Hampshire. Our duty is to follow close to these regiments, and when we get near enough each man is to throw his hand grenade over the parapet; then the regiments are to storm the works, and we are to follow and engage in hand-to hand conflict. There are 12 men taken from our company, 8 of whom are married.*

He continued in this very poignant missive:

> *We must have this place at any cost and, if I fall in this affair, my last thoughts shall be of you; and, if possible, I will request some friend to forward you this letter with my diary; but I hope to add more cheering intelligence. God shield me, and help me to do my duty!*

Three days later, under a flag of truce, a Rebel officer handed Wheeler's letter, which had been in the diary, to Lieutenant Colonel Wheelock Batcheller. A bullet had passed through letter and diary to Wheeler's heart. Wheeler's body was buried within the fort where he had climbed the parapet and met his death.[206]

The fort surrendered on July 8, 1863, only after Vicksburg surrendered to Grant. Banks lost his opportunity for a glorious victory in the west; nevertheless, the surrender opened up the Mississippi to the Union. But for the Twenty-Eighth, the cost was much more dear. As the men were shipped home, the town saw what the experience cost the men.

The Louisiana swamp took more lives than the battle of June 14— sunstroke, an unhealthy climate and foul water floating with animal carcasses and used as an open latrine by the soldiers made the two-month siege as unhealthy for the attackers as it was for those imprisoned in the fort. Soldiers of the Twenty-Eighth died in Louisiana and en route home, particularly along the Mississippi. Indeed, men continued to die after they returned home. The August 18, 1863 edition of the *Winsted Herald* stated:

> *The mortality which has prevailed among members of this regiment since its return from Port Hudson is truly frightful…we regret to observe that a fearfully large portion of those who thus sicken do not recover. One can almost recognize a Port Hudson man upon the street, by the lassitude, emaciation and debility he exhibits.*

One of those permanently disabled from this regiment was Cornelius Dayton, who, possibly for economic reasons and a sense of adventure, enlisted in Company F. Some things are worse than death. It is not known just when the family suspected that the Cornelius who returned was not the same healthy young man who had left less than a year earlier. When Chester Dayton, the soldier's father, filed for a pension based on his son's insanity in 1869, the affidavits by Dayton's superior, Second Lieutenant Jabez Alvord, claimed that he did not know that Dayton had ever been seen by a physician while in the service. The claim was apparently not approved. In 1871, after another petition from the father, Dr. James Welch, who had given Dayton his physical prior to entering the service, stated in a legal document that when Dayton returned he was suffering from chronic diarrhea and mental instability that had since increased until he was "perfectly insane." Alvord again testified that the reason Dayton hadn't been seen by a physician while in the service was that the only doctor had himself died while stationed at Port Hudson. First Lieutenant Caleb Newman also helped with the claim by stating, "Claimant was severely exposed to hard strife and suffering at and after the siege of Port Hudson." He added that "after such exposure Claimant seemed to become more careless and heedless of himself, and he gave evidence of mental disability beyond anything that had been observed before." This time, the claim was approved, and the family was awarded twenty-five dollars per month for the soldier's care (it ultimately rose to seventy-two dollars per month, one of the highest claims in the state).[207]

In 1882, Chester died, and the care of the unstable young man was transferred to Dayton's mother, Julia. Apparently, Cornelius could be a handful, as his volatile moods bordered on the dangerous, and he often tore his clothes from his body while in a rage. By 1901, when Julia's daughter,

Emma Dayton Marius, was widowed, the younger woman moved into the home to take care of her aging mother and brother. Several years later, Emma, a woman in her sixties, married Cornelius Andrus, a man half her age, apparently to help with her brother and her fragile mother, who was now half blind. Nevertheless, an investigation into his care resulted due to the lurid headlines in the December 28, 1910 issue of the *New York Times* that claimed that Dayton was "a dangerous maniac…[who] lived in a cage like a wild beast."

Emma Dayton as a young woman. In 1901, Emma moved back to her family home to take care of her aging mother and mentally unstable brother. *Dayton family donation.*

At the urging of Civil War veterans, the Connecticut Humane Society, which at that time investigated domestic abuse cases as well as animal abuse, had already investigated and found that the "cage" was actually a shed-like structure reinforced with barred windows. Agents Dwight W. Thrall of Hartford and John Simmons of Winsted found that Dayton paced his "cell" up and down, "carrying a spoon as he did his gun in the war." Dayton explained to the investigators that he was on guard duty. The agents found the room "scrupulously clean" and that he was being cared for "as well as possible under the circumstances." Nevertheless, in 1912, Julia A. Dayton resigned as guardian, with the paperwork noting the "pensioner" having been adjudged "incapable." Jonathan Marsh of Winsted was appointed conservator. Julia also turned over the property to his capable hands. Marsh did not serve as guardian long, as the *Winsted Evening Citizen* proclaimed on June 4, 1913, that "veteran rendered insane by sunstroke 49 years ago dead."[208]

Julia Dayton outlived her son. In 1916, headlines in the *Hartford Courant* proclaimed "Winchester Loses Oldest Resident." Nowhere in any of the newspapers was Cornelius Dayton ever mentioned in his mother's obituary. However, the *Winsted Evening Citizen* stated that the matriarch who died at the age of ninety-seven "lived a quiet life and was very devoted to her family." Her daughter, Emma, lived until 1933, and Emma's second husband, Cornelius Andrus, never remarried and died in 1961. The ripple effects of the Civil War on this family lasted almost a century.

COLD HARBOR

Probably the most horrific battle for Winchester and Litchfield County occurred on June 1, 1864. "It can almost be said that the 'heavens are hung in black,'" a dazed and grieving President Abraham Lincoln said upon viewing the long lists of dead and wounded from the killing fields of Cold Harbor, Virginia. Cold Harbor was not a single battle but rather a series of charges and skirmishes lasting from May 31 until Grant's retreat on June 12. Theodore F. Vaill, adjutant and historian of the Second Connecticut Heavy Artillery, wrote that the history books regard the June 3 battle when seven thousand men were wounded or killed in ten minutes as *the* Battle of Cold Harbor, yet, he continued, "that it always seemed…that the affair of June 1st was entitled to more than the two or three lines of bare mention with which it was tossed off." Rightly so, at least to the veterans and the families back home in the northwest corner of Connecticut whose sons fell in large numbers on that date.[209]

Almost two years earlier, Connecticut's Governor William Buckingham issued a proclamation ordering new regiments be formed to fulfill President Abraham Lincoln's request for more troops. By July 22, 1862, the people of Litchfield County had proposed that a regiment of soldiers be drawn exclusively from the ranks of men from the county, with towns setting $100 bounties to attract recruits. Company E of the newly formed regiment was recruited in Winsted. Thus, the Nineteenth Connecticut Volunteer Infantry (in a few years designated as the Second Connecticut Volunteer Heavy Artillery), affectionately known in the state as the Mountain County Regiment, was formed. The troops drilled at Camp Dutton in Litchfield for a month prior to mustering into the service of the United States for a period of three years on September 11, 1862.[210]

The Nineteenth's first assignment was picket duty in Alexandria, Virginia, a site that had fallen into Union hands in the first days of the war. The climate and foul water not being conducive to good health, numerous soldiers in the regiment, including Company E, sickened and died. Fortunately, within a few months, they were moved within the forts surrounding Washington, D.C., a more healthful and more relaxed climate. No longer needing to drill for duty at the front, they became quite proficient at handling the heavy artillery of the forts that they garrisoned. In November 1863, their designation was changed to Second Connecticut Volunteer Heavy Artillery (CVHA), and several officers were sent back to Connecticut to beef up the numbers of the regiment by 1,100 men to meet artillery regiment standards.[211] And yet the regiment was never used as heavy artillery.

General Ulysses S. Grant, after his stunning success on the Western Front, was ordered east in March 1864 to assume control of all the Union armies. The Overland Campaign, as the new strategy was named, followed territory familiar to veterans of the unsuccessful Peninsular Campaign led by General George B. McClellan two years earlier. Both McClellan and Grant were defeated repeatedly by the wily generals of the South. The "new" in the strategy was that Grant, unlike McClellan, would not retreat after the devastating losses but rather would continue on, pressing General Robert E. Lee's left flank, thus enabling the Union army—at least in theory—to get past Lee's army and move on to take Richmond. The deck, Grant knew, was stacked in his favor since his army vastly outnumbered Lee's. The plan only partially worked: Lee lost men he could not replace, but Grant lost many more men than Lee. On May 16, the call went out to strip the defenses of Washington, D.C. The heavy artillery units, including the Second Connecticut, were called to the front to meet their destiny.[212]

As the hungry, weary troops unused to marching—never mind hard marching—joined the Sixth Corp brigades at Cold Harbor, they noticed a great deal of activity around them. It had been decided to use the fresh "bandbox" troops of the Second Connecticut to lead the assault against the Rebels.[213]

Led by twenty-four-year-old Brigadier General Emory Upton, a favorite of General Grant's, the Heavies fell into line behind one of their own, Colonel Elisha Kellogg. Kellogg had fought at the same site two years prior at the Battle of Gaines's Mill and drew diagrams in the dirt to let his inexperienced troops know what to expect. When the call came to begin the attack at 5:00 p.m., Kellogg led the way, the first of the three lines of Heavies directly behind him. From left to right in the first line were Company A (Litchfield), Company B (Salisbury), Company K (composite of twenty-five towns) and, on the far right, Company E (Winsted). They covered half a mile of ground, sending back several hundred prisoners from captured Rebel rifle pits. Then they approached a hastily built barrier made of interlaced pine sprouts and saplings stretching about seventy feet long in front of the advancing Union line. Only two small paths intersected the barrier that would allow four men abreast to pass. As the Heavies tried to maneuver into these openings, the Rebels angled behind the breastworks and opened up with murderous crossfire.[214]

As the only regiment in the brigade to advance to the breastworks, the Heavies had all the Rebels guns aimed at them. As Vaill sadly recounted, "Our right was nobody's left, and our left was nobody's right." Kellogg, realizing the severity of the situation, shouted, "About face!" and was immediately struck by a fusillade of bullets, falling dead on the barrier. According to reports, over the din of 250 mangled, screaming men, the voice of Brigadier General Upton ordered, "Lie down." Probably never were men more eager to obey an order! They stayed in that position until they were able to retreat to their lines under the cover of darkness, and thus began the grim task of rescuing the wounded and retrieving the dead.[215]

About 140 men from Litchfield County had answered their last roll call that day, and many more were wounded. The county's casualties amounted to 3 percent of its male population. Of the numerous victims in Company E, which now included men from other towns, Winsted lost 11 men, including the young, well-liked Corporal James R. Baldwin and Private Henry C. Kent, who were missing and presumed dead. Quartermaster Sergeant James A. Green died a lingering death from a shot in the foot. The other soldiers who received fatal wounds—Corporals Frederick W. Daniels, Willard Hart and Alonzo J. Hull—died during the battle, as did Privates Alfred Comins, Lewis Downs, Walter Martin, Myron Ferris and John M. Teeter. Most are listed on the Non-Repatriated Monument at Forest View Cemetery in Winsted; all are listed on the marble tablets at the town's Soldiers' Monument. Elisha Kellogg's widow, a native of Winsted, had her husband's body brought home and interred at Forest View Cemetery. The entire county was in shock and mourning as the telegrams poured into the various towns, alerting them to the disastrous battle of June 1.[216]

On June 2, men throughout the Union army at Cold Harbor were busy sewing their names into their uniforms so that their bodies would be more readily identified in the battles ahead.

The next day, *the* battle of Cold Harbor began. The Eleventh CVI was in the field, part of the Eighteenth Corps. Company F's First Lieutenant Samuel B. Horne suffered two wounds within the hour. The painful shoulder wound made Horne's long overnight ride in a wagon over rutted roads to the field hospital an agonizing memory. "Pain, loss of blood and lack of food…made it the most wretched twenty-four hours in my army life," claimed Horne reminiscing. A few months later, he was promoted to captain of Company H.[217]

Behind the lines, bullets whizzed, and all were forced to keep their heads down. One who didn't was Corporal Albert Tuttle. In a letter to Albert's sister, Jenny, his captain offered his condolence and told her how her brother died: "He was looking over the Brest Works and was shot by a sharp shooter, was buried there and his grave was marked." Several days later, James Tuttle in the Fifth CVI heard about his brother's death from his father and replied in anger and sorrow:

> *I now seat myself to answer your most welcome though sorrowful letter which I have just received. It is hard to part with a brother clear but it cannot be helped. He should have been more careful....But I pity the first reb that runs across my rifle. I once had a brother in the army but have none now.*[218]

Cedar Creek/Petersburg

Under cover of darkness on June 12, the Union army marched toward Petersburg. Shortly after it arrived, the Second Connecticut Heavy Artillery was quickly moved from Petersburg to the nation's capital due to a threat by Confederate lieutenant general Jubal Early as he moved his troops toward Washington from the Shenandoah Valley. The assault was contained before the regiment arrived, but the exhausted troops were quick marched after Early in the army of General Phil Sheridan.

Union major general Phil Sheridan thought that after several hard-fought battles, the Confederates had left the Valley. He was mistaken. In the early morning of October 19, 1864, the Confederates attacked the sleeping Union army, capturing the Union pickets, which included Winsted's Henry Skinner. One of the first fatalities was Captain Benjamin Hosford of Winsted, shot in the head and instantly killed. William Addison Hosford, his brother and other members of Company D, according to adjutant Theodore Vaill, "carried the body about half a mile on the retreat, and were compelled to leave it there. At night it was found that the rebels had taken a ring from his finger, the straps from his coat, and the shoes from his feet."[219]

However, Early's men, jubilant in their apparent victory, decided to stop and eat breakfast in the Union camp. General Sheridan, who had been at a meeting, returned and had his men regroup. This time, the Union army cleared the Rebels from the Valley, which cut off much of the food supplies to the Confederate army. The Second Connecticut Heavy Artillery regiment was then ordered back to Petersburg.[220]

Meanwhile, three Black men—Edward Hazzard, his cousin Lewis Hazzard and Charles St. John, all originally from Winchester—had enlisted in the Twenty-Ninth Connecticut Volunteer Infantry, an all-Black regiment, although they signed from other towns since Winchester never openly recruited for this regiment. It had taken a while for Connecticut to enlist Black soldiers due to racism and paternalism, and the same held true, even though abolitionist sentiment was strong in the town of Winchester.

Early in 1861, the idea of arming Black soldiers was considered and discarded. Thomas M. Clarke of the *Winsted Herald* held a typically racist view expressed in an article on December 6, 1861. "The whole education of the slave is unmanly, unfitting him for fair, stand-up fight[ing]." He stated, "Our word for it, all the battles fought by negroes will be lost; all the forts garrisoned by them will be captured; and all the weapons placed in their hands will be considerably worse than thrown away, for the enemy will get them, cheap, and turn them against us."

In August 1862, an unidentified person from Winsted wrote to Governor William Buckingham, telling him that he was asked, apparently, numerous times by Black men who wished to be enlisted in a Black regiment. The governor carefully worded his reply, saying that a Black regiment being introduced into a White brigade would create "so much unpleasant feeling and irritation that more evil than good would result."[221]

Thomas M. Clarke moved away from his former position and agreed with Buckingham: "There is in many regiments an almost unanimous aversion to that kind of negro equality which must exist when both are brought into camp and into battle together."[222]

By December 12, 1862, some Black troops had been used, and General Butler and General Saxton lauded the armed former slaves. Saxton was quoted as saying that "they are obedient to orders, vigorous in attack, and in battle—they are trumps," adding that "I have always been a Democrat," as was Butler, "and I am not now an abolitionist, but I cannot help acknowledging the valor and capacity of these men. I tell you they would finish up the war themselves if they were given the opportunity to do it."[223]

At this point, agreement was coming together. On May 22, 1863, the official order, General Order No. 143, was issued giving details on how the United States Colored Troops would be organized (some states like Massachusetts were allowed to start recruiting earlier). Connecticut did not begin recruiting until the fall of 1863. Although Buckingham started recruiting in August, the Connecticut House did not give its approval until November. Many Black men did not wait for the state to begin recruiting, enlisting in Massachusetts and, in the case of Black Winchester patriots, enlisting in Rhode Island. Quickly, 10 percent of the enlisted men were Black, and they would suffer incredible casualties due to the Southern position that Black soldiers were not to be taken prisoner.

Eight days after the Battle of Cedar Creek, one of the many skirmishes occurred that ended the life of Lewis Hazzard and Charles St. John outside Petersburg. General Ulysses S. Grant's goal was to cut off all the railroad lines in the Petersburg hub, which directly led to Richmond. Before the winter of 1864–65, Grant wanted to capture a crucial railroad line, not only to work toward his goal but also for political reasons, to help President Lincoln in his election. While his army was moving in one direction, the troops closest to Richmond would move in a different direction as a distraction to stretch the Confederate lines behind their trenches as thin as possible. One of those regiments was the Twenty-Ninth Colored CVI. Its job was to skirmish with the farthest-forward Confederate pickets.

The men beat the pickets back to the first line of Confederate earthworks and held the pits for twenty-four hours, taunting the enemy, capturing or killing many while taking down the Rebel flag and hoisting up the Stars and Stripes. Unfortunately, the rest of the campaign did not go well for General Grant, and thus the Union regiments returned to their earthworks without the railroad line in their possession. The losses in the Twenty-Ninth included twelve members of the regiment, including the two from Winchester.[224]

One month earlier, the war ended for Samuel B. Horne of the Eleventh CVI. Although his recovery proceeded slowly from his wounds received at Cold Harbor, three months later and still considered an invalid, Lieutenant Horne returned to his regiment and served what was probably thought as light duty as an aide-de-camp to General Ord. Ten days later, at Chapin's Farm on September 29, 1864, this slight young man "while carrying an important message on the field was wounded and his horse killed; but not withstanding his severe wounds and sufferings, he continued on his way, delivered the order, and then joined his General but had to be taken to the rear on account of injuries received." In 1897, he was awarded the Congressional Medal of Honor.[225]

His work as a soldier was done, but Horne became a provost marshal in Richmond the following year after General Lee fled the city, pursued by the Union army, including the Second CVHA, to Appomattox Court House. The first troops in Richmond? Several companies of the Twenty-Ninth Colored CVI.[226]

Later in the year of 1865, Thomas M. Clarke sold the *Winsted Herald* to Joseph Vaill, and on January 1, 1866, the new editor, Theodore Vaill, the former adjunct of the Second CVHA, took up his pen to describe not the horrors of war but rather the early stages of the transformation of the village of Winchester to an economic powerhouse and the society it produced.

Chapter 10

CREATING THE "IDEAL TOWN"

The Naugatuck Railroad made its first run into Winsted on September 22, 1849. The railroad was chartered in 1845, with the railroad to be built between Bridgeport and Winsted. Construction began in April 1848 and was completed by May 1849. This was a big boost to Winsted's population, which grew by more than 65 percent between 1850 and 1860, bringing in more businesses and labor.[227]

Mary P. Hinsdale described the free excursion to Bridgeport for those in the region who had contributed as little as five dollars to the construction of the railroad:

> *Scores of people went who had never before seen a train of cars…we had a royal time, looking with wonder and delight at the pretty towns and villages and the finely built cars and crooked roadway which brought us to our journey's end in only four hours.*[228]

No longer was it necessary for the town's industries and farmers to transport their products to Canaan's Housatonic Railroad when the Naugatuck depot was centrally located in Winsted on Willow Street, which ran parallel to the Greenwoods Turnpike (Main Street). This encouraged businesses to develop in the central part of town. In 1854, the New England Pin Company was built by John G. Wetmore close by the depot on the corner of Bridge and Prospect Streets, and this gave the company easy access to the railroad. His invention of a new and improved machine to stick pins in their paper holders gave him an edge over his competitors, as they could not produce the nearly 11 million pins his company produced daily.[229]

The central point between West Winsted and the east village was known as "the Flats." Although Main Street went through the area, it had not been built up. Wetmore built the Opera House in 1872, locating it on the corner of Main and Elm Streets. Six years later, he opened the Winsted National Bank in the Opera House block. On the opposite side of Elm Street was the Clarke House Hotel. Wetmore built the Wetmore Block just west of the hotel and also attached to the Opera House on its east side another block. All were close to the depot and gave passengers, whether visiting tourists or businessmen, easy access to shopping, banking and entertainment.[230]

Improvements were made in the east village after Winsted was designated as a borough by the state legislature in 1858. William H. Phelps was chosen the first borough warden, a position similar to mayor. Phelps was born in Colebrook on April 5, 1818, to Dr. Lancelot Phelps, a prestigious doctor and U.S. Congressman, and his wife, Elizabeth Phelps. In 1840, William married Lucy Wakefield, the daughter of Dr. Luman Wakefield, who lived on the east side of the Winsted town Green.

William would take his knowledge of the dry goods business learned from his grandfather Alpha Sage and from the dry goods emporium of Normand Adams, where he served as clerk. That business was also located east of the Green, adjacent to the Winsted Hotel and the nearby Wakefield residence. In the 1840s, Phelps left for Chicago, where he formed a partnership in a mercantile firm. Nevertheless, he returned to Winsted in 1851 and purchased the magnificent Victorian fantasy on the west side of the town Green that he called Park Cottage, complete with gargoyles and a widow's walk. He became president of the Hurlbut Bank in 1854, a position he retained while also serving as the first warden.[231]

As warden, one of his first orders of business was to build sidewalks, improve streets and renovate the town Green. This lasting legacy was instituted not through taxes but by fundraising. He eliminated the road dividing the Green and built parallel roads. He then enclosed the park with stone and iron railings. Under his guidance, the park was graded and planted with grass and trees (prior to this the Green was not very "green," covered in gravel), and the entire area became known as Park Place.[232]

Slowly, a fire department began to emerge. In 1860, the state legislature gave the borough permission to take water from the lake. By 1862, the waterworks had tested the streams of water that could be thrown from the Green and the Flats, and it was concluded that the new hydrants (guarded by flour barrels to prevent people from hitching their horse to the hydrants) would be sufficient for fire protection. Gradually, and not without some rancor, the town divided itself into four fire districts and purchased four secondhand wheel carts for the fledgling department. Eventually, ladders and a bell were added. The first firemen's parade was established in 1867 in which the fire districts competed with one another by showing their prowess with the equipment.[233]

Although gas lines were put in place for streetlights almost immediately after Winsted became a borough, the quality was inconsistent. In 1874, an improved gas system was introduced, and more streetlamps were installed. However, by 1886, electricity was introduced to the town, albeit at a much higher cost, and gaslights were replaced with electric versions. In 1887, some of the stores on Main Street also had electric lights installed, which certainly helped retailers on Thursday evenings when they were open to encourage shoppers who had just received their pay packets.[234]

If a railroad running south from Winsted were able to bring about economic and population growth in Winsted, what would a second railroad running from Hartford to Millerton, New York, do for the towns where the line was laid? The public was very much in favor of an east–west railroad line, and in 1866, a charter was granted to the Connecticut Western Railroad Company. However, this had a shorter route than what was desired, starting in Collinsville and running to the Massachusetts border. Necessary railroad connections could not be made with other lines until the Dutchess and Columbia Railroad Company, with its connections to the Harlem Railroad in Millerton, New York, heard about the proposed Connecticut line. A new charter was arranged in the state legislature in 1868, with the stipulation that the Connecticut towns along the line, from Hartford to Millerton, subscribe in an amount not exceeding 5 percent of their grand list and with a vote at their town meetings approving the measure by a two-thirds majority. Winchester was the first town to pass the measure, promising $116,000 for stock in the line along with $74,900 in private subscriptions. Hartford, Bloomfield, Simsbury, Canton, Norfolk, Canaan and Salisbury followed suit.[235]

A number of businessmen were involved in harnessing community support. In addition, William L. Gilbert was elected to serve as a representative in the legislature for the 1868 term in order to make sure that the new charter was granted. Gilbert, as well as other businessmen in the town of Winchester, served on the railroad's board of directors, and Gilbert also served as the treasurer of the company. The railroad was not a moneymaker for its stockholders; the railroad would be absorbed by various other railroad companies throughout its existence, but Winsted became the most important railroad and industrial hub in northwest Connecticut.[236]

In June 1872, the Connecticut Western railroad delivered a shipment of 1 million bricks from Bloomfield. These bricks were used in construction projects that included the Beardsley Block at the west end of town, the new Music Hall/Opera House on the "Flats" in central Winsted and to replace William L. Gilbert's clock shop, in the east village, which had been destroyed by fire in 1871.[237]

Financing undoubtedly came from the banking industry in Winsted, which was controlled by the barons of business. Henry Gay had been the cashier of the ill-fated Winsted Bank that in 1861 was robbed of $60,000 via drilling through the floor of a vacant office above the vault. Although the suspects were caught, and one led officials to where some of the silver was hidden along the roadside to Norfolk, charges were never brought. When the Winsted Bank closed in 1867, William L. Gilbert joined the industry to add to his business portfolio. He and partner Henry Gay founded Gilbert & Gay. This new bank served business interests in town and in a new market: the West. In 1874, they closed the bank, as Gilbert was named president of the Hurlbut National Bank and Henry Gay his cashier. They would work together for the balance of Gilbert's life in various capacities.[238]

Henry Gay was William L. Gilbert's most trusted financial advisor in all things business, in which they were often partners, and carried out Gilbert's philanthropic concerns. *Connecticut Historical Society.*

If most of the successful businessmen could be considered barons, William L. Gilbert could be considered a king. Gilbert sought businesses that he felt would be successful in Winsted. One was the established business of Markham & Strong in East Hampton. Originally, the company made silver-plated bells, but it had moved into the lucrative coffin fixtures business after the Civil War. A joint stock company in Winsted led by Gilbert in 1866 provided the financing to bring the business to Winsted. The new company would be called the Strong Manufacturing Company, dealing in coffin trimmings of white metal, casket linings and shrouds.

For the first four years of its existence, Gilbert would be president. It wasn't until 1871 that David Strong; his brother, Clark; and brother-in-law, Henry G. Colt, would gain control of their company.[239]

When first organized, the business occupied a small wooden building near the corner of Rowley and Main Streets. A brick building was erected at the corner in 1873, and in 1866, the brick building was extended and the wooden building was torn down as orders for products escalated. Bells and coffin hardware plated with white metals soon evolved into a greatly extended line of elaborate coffin trimmings of silver and gold, as well as coffin linings and shrouds made with high-quality fabrics. Silver with gold nameplates for the coffins of Ulysses S. Grant, Benjamin Harrison and Cornelius Vanderbilt were some of the more noteworthy orders.[240]

Perhaps the Strong family chose their somewhat ghoulish occupation due to the family's experience with an abysmally high death rate in infant mortality and loss of spouse—actually much more reflective of seventeenth-century Jamestown than nineteenth-century New England. David Strong's grandfather lost eleven of nineteen children, and his aunt lost all nine of her infants within hours of their birth. David Strong himself married three times (his second and third wives were the Colt sisters, Maria and Emerette). He lost three children. Meanwhile, Clark lost two infants and a son just grown into young adulthood. And Clark himself lost his battle with consumption at an early age. Of David's three sons, only one had children.[241]

Clark's son Lester and David's three sons—Frederick, Herbert and Homer—continued the work in the family business. The families would all live an upper-middle-class lifestyle. They built homes on Walnut Street, as did David's brother-in-law, Henry G. Colt. Lester moved nearby on Holabird Avenue; a cousin, Anson Strong, lived on another street off Walnut, Grove Street. A friend, James. T. Morgan, who served as their foreman, also lived on Walnut Street. He opened Morgan Silver Plate Company in 1887 on Willow Street to complement Strong Manufacturing's offerings. All were an easy walk to work on Main Street.[242]

Another east village industry organized in 1882 by William L. Gilbert was the Winsted Hosiery, located on Whiting Street and Holabird Avenue in a three-story wooden structure. In August 1882, the firm was opened with a celebratory ball in the factory. Gilbert started the business as a small manufacturer of men's woolen hosiery, but as the market expanded, so did the business. When Gilbert died in 1890, David Strong took over the office of president in the firm. After Strong's death in 1914, Leverett W. Tiffany, who had served as secretary/treasurer under Gilbert and had opened a sales

Herbert Strong, son of industrialist David Strong, on his eighth birthday. As an adult, "Bert" would also work in the family business. *Connecticut Historical Society.*

office in New York City, was chosen as president. The company reached the pinnacle of its success under Edward B. Gaylord between the years of his presidency from 1929 to 1940, becoming the largest hosiery concern in the state by 1936.[243]

The successful start to the Winsted Hosiery encouraged the newly organized New England Knitting Mills to lease a building from the New England Pin Company in the center of town in 1887. Henry Gay was chosen as president, Edward B. Gaylord was secretary and treasurer and Leverett W. Tiffany was general manager. In 1899, Jay E. Spaulding, the president of the New England Pin Company, would serve as president of the knitting mill until his death in 1911, when Tiffany would take over serving both the hosiery and the knitting mill in that capacity simultaneously. Gaylord would also serve his presidency simultaneously at both factories from 1929 until 1940. As the company grew, it purchased real estate along Main Street. When the New England Pin Company was consolidated with the Star Pin Company of Derby and moved to that location in 1926, the New England Knitting Mills purchased all of its buildings and incorporated it into its rapidly expanding business.[244]

However, when *Connecticut Magazine* published an article in 1904 titled "Winsted the Ideal Town," it was not as much concerned with the numerous successful and diversified businesses as it was the philanthropy in the town.

The subscription library established in rooms in the Beardsley House in 1874 by Delia Rockwell Beardsley in honor of her husband, Elliott Beardsley, was running out of room. In 1895, the Ladies Library Association, headed by Mary P. Hinsdale, began to search for benefactors for a library building. Jennison J. Whiting, soap and candle manufacturer as well as hardware and variety store owner, stepped forward and purchased a lot on the corner of Main Street and Munro Place in 1897 for the construction of a new library building. Unfortunately, Mr. Whiting died before the building was completed, and the funds designated for its construction were not sufficient. Mrs. Whiting contributed the necessary amount, and the Beardsley Library moved into its new rooms in 1898. In 1899, the town appropriated annual funding to allow the library to become a public rather than a subscription library. The Memorial Library building had a separate board from the Beardsley Library until 1939, when an act of the state legislature allowed the two entities to combine under the name of the Beardsley and Memorial Library.[245]

The original impetus for a Soldiers' Memorial came from the local unit of the Grand Army of the Republic (GAR), Palmer Post No. 33 in Winsted. In 1870, a "People's Fair" brought in $1,078.09 for the erection of a monument in 1870. However, for almost two decades, bickering over the site—a not unusual problem in Winsted—kept the fundraising to a minimum. The editor of the *Winsted Herald* suggested that the "monument be mounted upon a two-yoke ox cart, then hauled up and down Main Street in order to satisfy the conflicting sentiments of the citizens."[246]

The GAR received a bequest of $1,000 from the estate of Francis Brown to be added to its fund in 1885. Interest on this amount was to be used annually to help needy widows and orphans of soldiers in the Civil War. The bequest itself was to be used once the monument was erected. In 1886, William L. Gilbert offered a donation of $4,000 to be added to the fund, but it was refused. This was not the first time a donation was refused—he had offered to help fund a high school in town, but it was not accepted. After the Civil War, he donated money to a freedmen's school in LaTeche, Louisiana. The recipients renamed the school the Gilbert Academy and Agricultural College and changed the name of the town to Winsted. Therefore, the offered donation to the Soldiers' Monument may have had some strings attached that were unacceptable to the GAR. Nevertheless, this offer spurred a chain reaction.[247]

In early April 1887, the GAR formed a committee to turn over the planning and funds collected thus far to the Winchester Soldiers' Memorial Park Association. This transfer was approved by the state legislature on April 27. John T. Rockwell, Caleb Camp and William L. Camp offered land at the top of Crown Street to the association with the condition that the building fund be increased to $7,000. The association—led by Henry Gay, banker, real estate mogul and close associate of Gilbert—promptly donated $4,000. Other town philanthropists quickly fell in line.[248]

No one contributed more to the monument than the widow of Francis Brown. Maria Brown offered $3,000 to pay the cost of its interior embellishments, including the marble mantel and marble tablets bearing the names of the more than three hundred men who represented Winchester during the war. Another $3,000 was donated for an arched granite portal that gave admittance to the Memorial Park grounds. In all, Mrs. Brown donated $14,000 to the erection of the monument, the park and its upkeep by her death in 1899.[249]

In addition to the monies that Maria Brown donated to the Soldiers' Monument and its park, she also left a generous bequest of $5,000 upon her

Soldiers' Monument at the turn of the century in a 1908 postcard. *Author's postcard collection.*

Maria Brown donated $14,000 to the erection and embellishment of the Soldiers' Monument park and provided a generous bequest to fund a hospital. *Connecticut Historical Society.*

death in 1899 to the Town of Winsted "to aid in furnishing a hospital." The drive to start a hospital was initiated by a young invalid, Adelyn Howard, who was bedridden but wanted to help the town get a hospital. She positioned a little bag on her bed to encourage her visitors to leave pennies for a hospital fund. Upon her death in 1898, the fund had garnered $250. Plans for a hospital had fired up the public, and in 1895, leaders from various towns in Litchfield County introduced a bill asking for $25,000 to build a public hospital in Winsted. The legislature approved the incorporation of the Litchfield County Hospital but denied the funds to build it. After Adelyn's death, the public decided to try again.[250]

In 1899, a new group called the Winchester Hospital Association, led by Dr. Edward H. Welch and Connecticut's Governor Lorrin A. Cooke, a Winsted resident, raised private funds, while Representative Elliot B. Bronson moved the bill to passage incorporating a hospital with an appropriation of $10,000. A potential problem resulted. Two groups were incorporated to build a hospital. A few months later, the groups merged and became the Litchfield County Hospital of Winchester, with Dr. Welch as president, while the governor became president of the incorporating board.[251]

Susan Maria Brown Perry donated money for a "free bed" at the hospital. Another project, senior housing, was realized after the turn of the twentieth century. *Beardsley family files.*

In addition to the funds from Howard and Brown, Julia Batcheller, former owner of the Thayer Scythe Company, gave the hospital the land at the top of the cobble and additional monies to grade the property. Susan M.B. Perry, Maria Brown's daughter, gave $5,000 for a "free" bed. Other persons gave between $100 to $40,000 to the fledgling hospital. In 1912, more money, public and private, was raised for a twenty-room nurses' residence, and Wheelock Batcheller donated $7,000 for an isolation unit, which replaced the "pesthouse" on Wallen's Hill. This was built, fortuitously, before the Spanish flu epidemic in 1918.[252]

William L. Gilbert, born to a poor farmer in Newfield, went into the teaching field but found the pittance paid not to his liking. During his rise as an industrialist, he resented talk that he "made" money; instead, he claimed that he "saved" money. Indeed he did. For years, he was looked on as a miser. One contemporary remembered him as loving money "with a devotion approaching to idolatry, was close-fisted, made hard bargains, and was meanly economical." When asked by a delegation of his workers for a raise, he told them they shouldn't have so many children. For his household of four—which included, his wife, a niece and a maid—he allowed only one pint of milk be purchased per day. He stinted on himself as well. He wore neat but very worn clothes, and his horse and buggy were "disreputable." At one time, he moved to a town near New London, where he would pay lower taxes, until his business partner, Henry Gay, told him that it was unseemly. On a business trip with Mr. Wheeler, who was the traveling salesman for the Strong Manufacturing Company, Gilbert criticized Wheeler for spending a dollar for a peach. "Mr. Gilbert, I have been selling shrouds for twenty-five years, and I never yet sold one with a pocket in it." A little food for thought for Mr. Gilbert.[253]

As he neared the end of his life, Gilbert was encouraged by Henry Gay, his business partner and conscience, to consider how he was to leave his fortune. The three major charities that Gilbert provided the town—the Gilbert Home for Friendless Children, an orphanage (1889); the Gilbert School, a semi-private high school (1895); and the improvements to Winsted's waterworks—could not have happened without Gay.

Gay purchased the land for the Gilbert Home from his own pocket. Gilbert's plan was to construct the first building and wanted it to be wooden and of cheap materials. Gay resorted to recruiting other leaders to mention to Gilbert in passing that the children's home would be a lasting monument to him, so it would be unfitting to make it of anything but of sturdy brick. It was built of brick. That was easy compared to making the Gilbert School a reality. First, he had to purchase the land with $20,000 from David Strong and other wealthy citizens, then have the buildings, which included the Winsted Hotel, moved to the south side of Main Street, where it was renamed the Park Hotel. He also had to draw up a will for Gilbert, which was signed a mere four months before Gilbert's death. Finally, the waterworks were a near miss for the town. Upon hearing that Gilbert was near death during Gilbert's visit to Ontario, Canada, Henry Gay boarded a train and added a codicil adding $48,000 for the water project, which Gilbert signed on June 11, 1890. Gilbert died in Canada on June 29. The bulk of the more than $1 million in his will went to provide additional funds to the Home and the Gilbert School, plus $40,000 for the Gilbert Academy in Louisiana. His nephews contested the will (Gilbert's second wife died in 1889, and his children had died decades earlier), but the court found the will airtight.[254]

Ironically, William L. Gilbert, at one time considered the town's greatest miser, thanks to the dedication, guidance and financial acumen of his closest friend, Henry Gay, became heralded as the town's greatest benefactor.

Chapter 11
"THE LAKE'S THE THING"

In addition to the water from Highland Lake flowing down the lake stream to drive the scores of waterwheels that propelled Winsted's industries by the mid-nineteenth century, a number of less well-known businesses were derived from Winchester's water sources. Sawmills, especially those at Long Lake (Highland Lake), started a necessary lumber industry. Without sawmills to cut and plane wood into planks, businesses and homes would have been built of logs.

A byproduct of a growing lumber business was the introduction of charcoal kilns by 1833 to serve the mining industries in western Connecticut and as a heating source. Charcoal was considered efficient and environmentally friendly since the heat produced was twice as much as the same weight in wood. But within a few years, the heating requirements and the kilns of Kent and Salisbury had denuded the trees from the towns of western Connecticut by the 1850s. And it was potentially dangerous, as testified to by Mary Hinsdale, who witnessed this fire at the head of the lake:

> *There were three charcoal kilns just at the head of the pond, and men were also burning charcoal at the lower shores. Houses for storing charcoal were stationed at different places on Mill Hill, as Lake Street was then called, and the burning of one of them in the night was an incident in memory. The fierce heat of burning charcoal, the extreme cold weather, the bucket brigade of men (for there was no fire engine), the cooking of sausages and making coffee and the ice-covered and ice-cold men passing in and out were stories told over again and again in the home.*[255]

Another business that received short shrift in the annals of the town were the icehouses, a necessity for the preservation of food and dairy that stretches back millennia. Icehouses possibly started on water sources in Winchester other than on Highland Lake. William F. Hatch lived near Crystal Lake, then called Little Pond, and was the founder of the ice business in town, which he ran as a wholesaler and retailer, possibly as early as 1840. This business may have started as a side business to his agricultural pursuits, for he was long regarded a leading agriculturist of the region and was for many years secretary and treasurer of the Greenwoods Agricultural Society. Elevating agricultural science was his aim. And he realized that ice was instrumental in keeping produce and dairy fresh.[256]

William F. Hatch was a leading agriculturalist whose introduction of the ice business, possibly as early as 1840, allowed for the preservation of food and dairy. *Connecticut Historical Society.*

Other farmers, like Lester Hurlbut, who began a dairy farm in 1910 on South Road, blocked up a dam along a brook on his property; in February, the ice was harvested. February was chosen since ice, at a minimum, had to be at least eight inches in depth to last through the summer. Farmers exchanged labor for ice, cutting the blocks of ice and storing it in icehouses, packing sawdust around the blocks of ice to keep it from melting. This was crucial to dairy farmers, who needed to keep their milk cool for shipping to Hartford.[257]

However, the influx of potential consumers in Winsted who needed ice to preserve their food was a welcome source of additional income for farmers and other businessmen. Highland Lake therefore became the source of ice for much of the city and beyond. The largest number of commercial icehouses was located on the northern end of East Lake Street. This was a large winter business, with names of ice dealers like John and Lawrence Hannon, Thomas Hannafin, William E. Bull and the partnership of Bradley Dewy and Elizur B. Parsons. Some may have just sold ice at retail; others, like the Hannons, were wholesalers who stocked the retail businesses and were retailers themselves.

The Hannons owned four icehouses; several were tall wooden buildings that had conveyor belts or pulleys outside that dragged the huge ice blocks and deposited them within the buildings. One of these icehouses had been purchased from E.B. Parsons, who in 1896 left the ice business as his building contracting business was booming. The Hannons sold lumber as part of their business and rented boats to tourists during the summer months, as ice harvesting was a risky business and was not reliable income by itself. The boathouses were lodged between the icehouses but could be moved when necessary.[258]

Warm winters sometimes occurred at the worst times, as one did during a recession in 1857–58, when William Hatch began to worry there would be no ice harvest just when people could least afford to let food spoil. Fortunately, the very warm winter of 1890 occurred a few years prior to a major recession. That warm-up was reported by the *Winsted Herald* at the end of February to have taken "all hope out of the ice men, and for that matter out of everybody, for everybody is solicitous lest there may be an ice famine." An ice famine meant no shipping of milk to New York and other cities, which would hurt Winchester's dairy industry, and there would be no ice for iceboxes to preserve food in Winsted. The fear of an ice famine caused inventors and entrepreneurs to design and promote the manufacturing of ice.[259]

Some households had electric refrigeration by the time the next really warm winter occurred, during the Great Depression in the winter of 1931–32. The Hannons decided to build an ice manufacturing plant on the edge of Highland Lake that would make ice on demand. It was insulated against heat and cold. However, within a few years, once people could afford refrigerators, the icehouses became redundant. Most were either taken down or repurposed.[260]

As important as the lake was to the growth of rural Winchester and the growing borough of Winsted, a descendant of Eliphaz Alvord, Coridon Alvord, a New York City book publisher, wrote a letter to the *Winsted Herald* that noted that the town was missing the point: "The lake is the thing….No shore resort on Long Island Sound could compare with it." He suggested the formation of a $60,000 corporation to purchase the land around the lake in a strip a half mile wide with the plan to build a boulevard one hundred feet wide. A landscape engineer should be secured to groom and plant the area appropriately to make it a "splendid resort."[261]

The seed of the idea was planted, but nothing further happened for ten years. In 1884, a retired and sickly Harvey Wakefield was living on Main Street in Winsted. Wakefield, who was born to Aden and Susannah Wakefield of Colebrook in 1802, had married Eliza Barber in 1853. Harvey and Eliza lived on the farm with his aging parents until after their deaths in 1856 and '57. At that point, Harvey and Eliza moved to Winchester to work their own farm.

Henry Gay was Wakefield's financial advisor. At Gay's urging, Wakefield, now a widower, made his will. After generous bequests to several churches in Winsted, the balance of $11,855.25 was left to the Town of Winchester. This was enough to build a boulevard around Highland Lake that some in (and out of) the community had been urging for a decade.[262]

As it happened, it took several years to complete the road, which turned out to be more a wide path than a boulevard, yet it allowed access to the lake at a propitious time. Once the water supply of the town's drinking water was changed from Highland Lake to Crystal Lake in 1895, thanks to the gift of William L. Gilbert, the lake could be more fully utilized for recreation.

Recreation in the area had begun in the 1880s in the paths and woodlands around the lake on the east side. On the lake itself, passenger boats— including the steamboats the *Iron Clad*, *Tunxis*, *Blanche*, *Highland* and the *Carrie*—were used to move passengers from the spillways to points along the lake, particularly Hatch's Landing. This was the boat landing site for the Highland Lake Transportation Company's day resort, Highland Park, on the southern end of the eastern portion of third bay.

The company built a dining and dance hall, while a generator supplied lights, giving the name "Electric Park" to the venture. An artistic brochure distributed by the company, "A Day's Outing by Rail and Water," described the delights that awaited the day-tripper, especially at the end of the day:

> *Upon a quiet evening, when the scene bears an aspect of deep seclusion and tranquility, when the great luminary has dropped behind the western hills, and the heavens one blaze of glory mirror a resplendent expanse in the flood, mingling the crimsons of sunset with the deep blue shadows of the hills, then, indeed Highland Lake is to be seen in all its beauty.[263]*

Unfortunately, the original park only lasted two years. Although the much-touted accessibility to Winsted via train and then, once at Highland Lake, via boat to the park was much appreciated, the deal-breaker may have been the steep ten-minute walk up to the lake, which was about one hundred feet above the city. Nevertheless, in 1897, a trolley line was established by the Connecticut Company between Torrington and Winsted, and immediately afterward, a spur from Burrville was established over Case Mountain to Electric Park, which then established itself as the "Little Coney Island."

An 1890 Highland Transportation Company brochure introduced the middle-class day-tripper to the pristine beauty of Highland Lake. *Beardsley Library.*

Highland Lake has three bays. This is the first bay. *Author's postcard collection.*

Added to the pavilion and dining room was a bathhouse; a candy stand; an ice cream parlor; a wooden slide (called a roller coaster), which dumped the person, seat and all, into the lake; a shooting gallery; and a merry-go-round. Boating was encouraged.[264]

In 1926, Woodland Park—a similar day resort with roller skating, dancing, swimming and a high diving board—was established by Gaetano Lentini at the northern head of the lake near the spillways. This was a year before trolley service to Winsted was eliminated. Both parks carried on as the road around the lake, as well as boating on the lake, continued to allow visitors and those property owners fortunate enough to own lakefront property to make memories at the lake.[265]

Almost simultaneously with the opening of Highland Park, the first owner of a summer cottage along the boulevard was William L. Camp, who built his cottage on the west side in third bay in the late 1880s. This house would be purchased, enlarged and then opened in July 1900 as the Highland Lake Hotel. In 1919, the hotel was sold to Mrs. Margaret Fjelde and renamed the Hiawatha Lodge. The lodge was destroyed by fire in 1929. In 1905–6, the Lakeview Inn was located at 228 East Lake Street near the spillways. In 1907, the owner, Eliphalet Hall, joined with Dudley J. Paine as proprietor of the Beardsley House in Winsted. Although there was talk and even offerings

Boating at Highland Lake has always been a delightful pastime for pleasure and business. *Author's postcard collection.*

of property to accommodate a hotel, the private property owners were less than welcoming of the idea.[266]

Land on the west side of the lake, much of which had been owned by Rufus Holmes for his Highland Farm property, sold quickly when broken into lots for cottages. On the east side, contractor Joseph Carey, who had purchased much of the land from the Case family, sold 640 acres to the Highland Lake Development Company in 1927, which caused a housing boom around the lake. By 1971, there were more than six hundred cottages. Although, at first, many of these cottages were for summer use only, as the years went by many were enlarged and winterized, making a year-round community.[267]

By the 1950s, Highland Park had been allowed to deteriorate, and when the pavilion was destroyed by fire, the property was sold for more cottage lots. In the 1960s, Woodland Park was offered for sale to the town, but taxpayers refused the offer. It was then offered to the state, which purchased it for a state boat launch.[268]

There are two small beaches—one on the northeast side of the lake, Resha Beach, and on the northwest side, Holland Beach—which are accessible to the town's residents. The drive around Highland Lake, though not as open to viewing as it once was, is still glorious, especially at dawn and sunset. And on an early spring or sunny, late summer day, the lake—"a sheet of crystal, framed in a ring of greenery; overhead…white fleecy clouds, that lie like freighted ships at anchor, or sail slowly above through the still air"—still cries, "The lake's the thing!"[269]

Chapter 12

THEY PUT WINSTED "ON THE MAP"

Winsted's social and cultural life was on the upswing almost immediately after the Civil War. People did not spend all their time making money or talking business, as Edmund C. Stedman had complained in the 1850s. Due in part to its location as a railroad hub, with a thriving middle class, Winsted was part of a vast lecture and entertainment circuit, but it also attracted cultural luminaries who, for a time, made Winsted their home. And one Winsted native refused the offers from larger cultural centers, preferring to remain in his hometown.

ROSE TERRY COOKE

In January 1881, a gala was presented at the Opera House to raise funds for a reading room in the East village. Rose Terry Cooke (1827–1892) supervised the production, whose star of the evening was her dear friend Mark Twain, who performed his amusing readings and anecdotes.[270]

Of Mrs. Cooke, a speaker at a 1913 Connecticut Historical Society event declared, "In determining the rank among the writers of our country should be accorded Rose Terry Cooke to claim a place for her among the ablest. John G. Whittier gave her the precedence over Harriet Beecher Stowe in the use of the New York dialect and declared her without equal in her stories of New England life."[271]

Rose Terry Cooke purchased the old manse built in 1795 by Jenkins and Boyd along the Still River. She took great pride in her garden, filled with eighteenth-century flowers. *Connecticut Historical Society*.

As a youth, Rose Terry attended Catherine Beecher's Hartford Female Seminary. She assumed the role of teacher and governess but in 1847 returned to Hartford to begin her literary career. Her writings appeared in all the major periodicals of the time, including *Putnam's* and *Harper's*. She was only one of two women invited to appear in the first issue of the *Atlantic Monthly* in November 1857.[272]

In 1873, at the age of forty-six, Rose Terry married Rollin H. Cooke, a bank clerk in Winsted. They first lived in an apartment in the Opera House and then moved to Walnut Street. However, she had fallen in love with the house, built in 1795 by Jenkins and Boyd, the Winsted scythe makers, on North Main. She bought the house and restored it and its garden. Her garden, according to the *Boston Evening Record* of 1886, was "an ample and most attractive old-fashioned garden. This full of hollyhocks, old-fashioned white roses, sweet peas, geraniums, phlox, honey-suckles, trumpet vine and the thousand and one old-time flowers used to so adorn our grandmothers—is the delight of Mrs. Cooke."[273]

Her writing included stories and poems, primarily on rural New England life, for which she was able to draw from abundant material of tales in various towns, especially in Winsted. Titles include *Huckleberries: Gathered from New England Hills*, a volume that includes the short story "An

Old-Fashioned Thanksgiving," which came about after the story regarding Hannah Everett's experience in the American Revolution came to light in John Boyd's *Annals*, published in 1873. Her personal favorite short story was "The Deacon's Week," which she wrote after an "energetic" discussion with a parson in the borough.[274]

An article entitled "Mytown," which is a thinly disguised ode to the town of Winchester and its many attractions, was printed in *Harper's* in October 1877. Here she refrained from the use of New England dialect, instead using elegant prose bordering on the poetic to discuss the businesses of Winsted and its beautiful urban and rural features:

> *The observant eye is amused to see orthodox posts and lanterns on one side of the pavement, and long wreaths of blackberry and trailing garlands of clematis on the other, while from these traces of high civilization, you can, in five minutes' walk, plunge into fragrant depths of forest, or climb to heights of rugged granite, from whose pinnacles or precipices, you "view the landscape o'er."[275]*

It was very difficult for her when, in 1887, her husband took a different banking job in Pittsfield, Massachusetts, after his risky investment in his father's company ruined them. She had truly loved her home on the banks of the Still River and her adopted town. She died five years later.

SARAH E. HARVEY

Although Cooke painted with words, folk artist Sarah E. Harvey (1834–1924) painted with the brush. A contemporary of Cooke's, Harvey, born in Colebrook just a few miles north of Winsted, never received formal instruction in painting. That did not stop her, since by her own estimation, she completed at least one thousand pictures over a career of more than six decades, all but one hundred given to family and friends.[276]

Her paintings ran the gamut from landscapes and mourning paintings featuring urns to still lifes and at least one self-portrait. Although the furthest she traveled from her New England roots was for her first marriage in Washington, D.C., to Lieutenant Jules DeCroy during the Civil War, she copied "photographic sources of places in Europe and the tropics to paint her idealized versions." Her medium was not always canvas, for she also painted on wood, porcelain and even a stovepipe.[277]

Winsted, Connecticut, ca. 1877 is one of many thousands of works painted by folk artist Sarah E. Harvey, who for many years resided in Winsted. *Princeton University Museum Collection.*

Shortly after the war, the Parisian-born DeCroy died, and the widowed DeCroy remarried in 1868 to Edward Horrigan of Tolland, Massachusetts. The family moved to Winsted, where Harvey painted local scenery, homes and businesses. Harvey has been described by those who knew her as "a diminutive, yet fascinatingly intriguing woman with a delightful sense of humor"; she was credited with "a great joy and zest for living."[278]

Harvey's masterpiece was her folk art landscape of the east village of Winsted titled *Winsted, Connecticut, ca. 1877,* housed in the Princeton University Art Museum. The eighteen-by-twenty-eight-inch oil on canvas painting, as analyzed by the art museum, "{is} rendered with such precision that individual buildings…are clearly identifiable, including St. Joseph's Church and Monastery at left and, most prominently, at far right, the Strong Manufacturing Company, makers of gilded coffin hardware." David Strong's Victorian mansion on Walnut Street is also included in the painting, slightly above the center of the work. It is distinguished by the two trees in the yard obscuring some of the detail.[279]

T.M.V. DOUGHTY

The Strong home, built in 1869, is also featured in a stereograph photographed by the studio of T.M.V. Doughty. Thomas Moses Vaill Doughty (1824–1911) was born in Union Vale, New York. As young man, he was a store clerk and a teacher in Cornwall, as well as served as a clerk in the old Hurlbut store in Winchester Center. In his early twenties, he and his brother, John, supported themselves as artists. But before long, he went to New York City and received daguerreotype instruction from one of the earliest photographers in the United States, Seth Catlin Landon.[280]

Within a short time, Landon moved to Winsted and opened the Sunshine Daguerreian Gallery, while his student owned and operated a Daguerreian wagon in Lakeville, Connecticut. However, in 1856, Doughty purchased the

Opposite: This is one of T.M.V. Doughty's photograph studios of the 1850s and '60s, located on the corner of Bridge and Main Streets. He later moved his business to Union Street. *Connecticut Historical Society*.

Above: David Strong House stereograph by T.M.V. Doughty—one of many stereographs done by Doughty of Winsted. *Getty Museum*.

gallery from Landon. During the 1850s and '60s, he operated two studios on Main Street, one in the back of the Hurlbut bank and the other in a brick block on the corner of Main and Bridge Street. He had several assistants whom he trained in the art, including his wife, Elizabeth; his brother, Edgar; and his brother-in-law, King T. Sheldon. Doughty was eager and willing to share his knowledge of his craft with others and was a frequent contributor to the *British Journal of Photography*.[281]

Daguerreotypes began to fall out of favor as the art and science of photography advanced. During the Civil War, Doughty specialized in *cartes de visite*, small 2.5-by-3.5-inch photographs printed on paper and mounted on a slightly larger, heavier paper. These became extremely popular during the Civil War, when soldiers gave them to their friends and family and, in particular, traded them with other soldiers. Another specialty was the stereograph. Doughty took two nearly identical photographs with a special camera. Printed side by side and viewed through a stereoscope, the view appeared as a three-dimensional image. Many families spent their evenings viewing series of related cards, sold together in themed packets. The idea is very similar to that of the twentieth-century View-Master.[282]

Although many of Doughty's subjects for stereographs were of scenes and houses, the bulk of his work was portraiture. Most nearby successful businessmen, men in the professions and their wives had their photographs taken in his studio. He was so successful that he built and moved into a new, larger studio on Union Street, where he continued his business until he retired in 1910.[283]

KING T. SHELDON

King Sheldon learned the craft of photography from his brother-in-law, T.M.V. Doughty. He specialized in events, natural disasters and celebrations. *Connecticut Historical Society.*

King T. Sheldon (1846–1912), Doughty's brother-in-law, specialized in events, scenes and landscapes in his photographic career. King followed his sister and Doughty to Winsted at the age of sixteen and lived with the family until his marriage in 1872. He opened his own studio on Main Street in 1870, but when the former Higley Tavern property became available (the tavern had already been dismantled), Sheldon purchased a portion of the land and built a two-story building for his new photographic gallery.[284]

Some of Sheldon's most memorable photographs are from the 1876 centennial celebration, the 1882 Winsted cyclone and the blizzard of '88, as well as scenes of devastation from fires that plagued the town. One of the worst fires occurred in 1889, destroying Camp's Block at the corner of Main and Lake Streets, along with J.J. Whiting's Variety Store building and Apothecaries' Hall. It also badly burned Sheldon's studio. He repaired his studio and remained in that location until his death.[285]

John G. Doughty/Alfred E. Moore

John G. Doughty (1858–1910), son of T.M.V. Doughty, was born not long after the family moved to town. His experience in his father's studio had him choosing photography as a vocation, but it took him in a new direction: up!

The most famous of Winsted's aeronauts was industrialist Alfred E. Moore, whose wealth enabled him to take up the expensive hobby of ballooning. On July 29, 1885, Moore and another well-known Connecticut aeronaut, Silas M. Brooks, made a balloon ascension from Winsted, Connecticut, in a balloon named "Winsted." The 80-foot-high balloon had a circumference of 120 feet. Rain, however, dampened the experience. As the aeronauts let the gas out of the balloon, the wildly swaying balloon bumped along the ground upon landing. A New York newspaper claimed that the two aeronauts "lost their hold on the slippery rail and fell headlong from the car…the crowds did their best to catch the aeronauts as they fell. Brooks was badly hurt. He is expected to die." The *Winsted Herald* mocked the New York newspaper for not letting the facts get in the way of a sensational story, yet that was the story that unfortunately went nationwide. Neither man "fell from the balloon," and Brooks lived another twenty-one years.[286]

John Doughty was invited to make the next ascension with Moore to take photographs. Moore had constructed the balloon to carry three persons along with balloonist's equipment, such as sandbags for ballast and a grappling hook or anchor to slow and stop a balloon during descent. He had also designed the balloon's basket with a square hole in the bottom to enable a photographer to take pictures looking straight down.

Doughty had made photographs of the July flight from the ground looking upward. He was a little apprehensive about actually leaving the safety of the earth to take photographs looking down. Upon completing the September 2, 1885 flight whose altitude reached an estimated seven thousand feet, Doughty exclaimed, "No one who ever thinks of making an ascension can possibly dread the experience more than I did, and revulsion of feeling

Left: John G. Doughty was the son of T.M.V. Doughty. His photographic specialties were of balloon ascensions from the ground and from thousands of feet above the earth. *Connecticut Historical Society*.

Below: Alfred E. Moore, the Winsted balloonist, is the second from the right. It is believed that John G. Doughty took the photograph. *Connecticut Historical Society*.

which took place when the ascension was made, and I at last found myself where I had feared to be—higher than the clouds!"[287]

No photographs were taken on this first flight, as the wind kept them from making their ascent until 5:00 p.m., when the sunlight was not good for proper exposure of the sensitive plates. Nevertheless, Doughty experimented with the camera and gear to enable him to offset the challenges of flying, such as the slow rotating motion of the balloon. It also enabled Doughty to perfectly calculate the conditions for the next flight they took together, in mid-October, to take a series of photographs starting in Winsted and including photographs of various towns, including Simsbury and Windsor, from altitudes often exceeding five thousand feet.[288]

The final flight they made together was made on June 17, 1887, from Sportsman's Park, St. Louis, under the auspices of the *New York World*, which paid for the new balloon and its basket. Joseph Pulitzer had purchased the newspaper four years earlier and had recently purchased a share of the *St. Louis Post Dispatch*. He hoped to promote his newspaper by creating excitement akin to that of Jules Verne's *Around the World in 80 Days* with an aerial stunt joining St. Louis with Manhattan using a hot air balloon. On the "transcontinental trip," they were to drop thousands of flyers extolling the *New York World* as the leading morning newspaper of America and the *St. Louis Post-Dispatch* as the leading evening newspaper.

This was not the goal of H. Allen Hazen of Washington, who worked for the U.S. Signal Service and whose intent was to prove that the air currents traveled easterly. The goal was to land somewhere on the Atlantic seaboard. He traveled with Moore, Doughty and *World* reporter Edward Duffy. In the late afternoon, they left. One estimate was that they reached sixteen thousand feet, but the balloon was unmanageable and a dangerous landing was made in Illinois, fifty-five miles northeast of St. Louis. Therefore, the ascent was a failure from the newspaper's point of view. Pulitzer was more successful two years later when using other forms of transport to send reporter Nellie Bly on an around-the-world junket.[289]

Nevertheless, Hazen's report to the Signal Service was that the flight was successful from a scientific point of view. Moore died three years later of Bright's disease, but the basket that he made for the 1887 journey was displayed in the family's front yard on Main Street for years.

FRANK DEMARS

Frank DeMars (1872–1942), born in the Robertsville section of Colebrook, had the fortunate experience of being quite successful at everything he did, whether it was as a photographer, as a chronicler of the town's history or as an advocate for his community. At times, he was able to combine the three.

DeMars spent most of his life in Winsted and, while still attending school, sold Burpee seeds and fruits and vegetables from his father's garden. He received a paycheck from the Boston Store on Main Street and did odd jobs in Winsted and nearby communities. However, by the turn of the century, he had begun to settle in earnest into the career of a photographer, just as rural aspects of Winsted were gradually being lost to modernity. His photographs recorded Winsted-area homes, businesses, town streets and landscapes— encouraged by Winsted's other high-profile photographers. Indeed, he began to purchase their glass plate negatives. He became the proprietor of the Art Store, which featured framing and where he sold postcards of the images that he and other area photographers had produced.[290]

Postcards were introduced at the Columbian Exposition of 1893, and like the advent of the stereopticon and the photograph album, they created a sensation. Few homes were without the postcard album, and the weary traveler was warned not to return home without first having mailed postcards to his album-keeping friends. By 1908, DeMars, with help from

Frank DeMars was a photographer, art dealer, chronicler of the town's history and advocate for the town. *Connecticut Historical Society.*

his wife and children, was putting the final touches on his black-and-white photographs, printing them in his attic on a printing press that had belonged to his mother. The finished product was then sent to Germany to be colorized and printed. In 1914, he sold the business but continued to independently produce postcards while restarting a business as a horticulturalist.

DeMars sold plants, did landscape gardening and put in gardens for others. He also was very involved with the community, starting the Parent-Teachers Organization in schools in town, and as a "cheer-leader" for the town he spoke to the Rotary Club and advised it that "Winsted's Diamond Mine" was the mountain laurel. He claimed that

Winchester had the largest crop in the world nearby. He then went on to promote and receive the designation of "Winsted, the Laurel City" from the state legislature. As the first president of the Laurel City Horticultural Society, he advocated for a "Laurel Week" in June. Two years later, in June 1934, the crowning of the first Laurel Queen tradition commenced with the first queen, Gladys Weaving, selected by students at the Central School on Wetmore Avenue and crowned by author and avid gardener Ruth Cross. DeMars's own crowning achievement was *Winsted and the Town of Winchester*, taking up the written history of the town from where John Boyd concluded. This massive undertaking was completed after his death by Elliott P. Bronson in time for the town's bicentennial in 1971.

Mattie Ruth Cross

Mattie Ruth Cross (1887–1981) was born in Sylvan, Texas. She enrolled at the University of Texas and worked her way through college by teaching in small towns. She didn't graduate with her degree in creative writing until 1911, possibly due to her finances, as well as an eye malady that required someone to read and take notes for her.

Eleven years after she graduated, she finally sold her work to a literary magazine. Then, in 1922, Louis B. Mayer based a movie on one of her short stories. Two years later, her first novel, *The Golden Cocoon*, struck pay dirt—not only as a literary effort but also as a film produced by Warner Bros. in 1925. She received $25,000 for the rights.[291]

A year earlier, Ruth (she did not use the name Mattie) married horticulturalist and financier George W. Palmer. In August 1924, they took a trip to Connecticut and traveled down a country road just outside the city of Winsted. "We had been warned never to look at a place in New England in apple blossom time, laurel time, nor when autumn had emptied her paint pots over the land. But September caught us napping." Soon they were the proud owners of forty acres and a house in such disrepair that they weren't sure they would be able to live in it.[292]

Over the next few years, they altered their paradise, changing the location of shrubs, trees and planting gardens to gain the most artistic views possible, as well as totally reconstructing the house, which she named Edendale. They built a garage out of debris but refused to remove the apple tree that stood where they needed the garage. They built around it. After all, what Eden

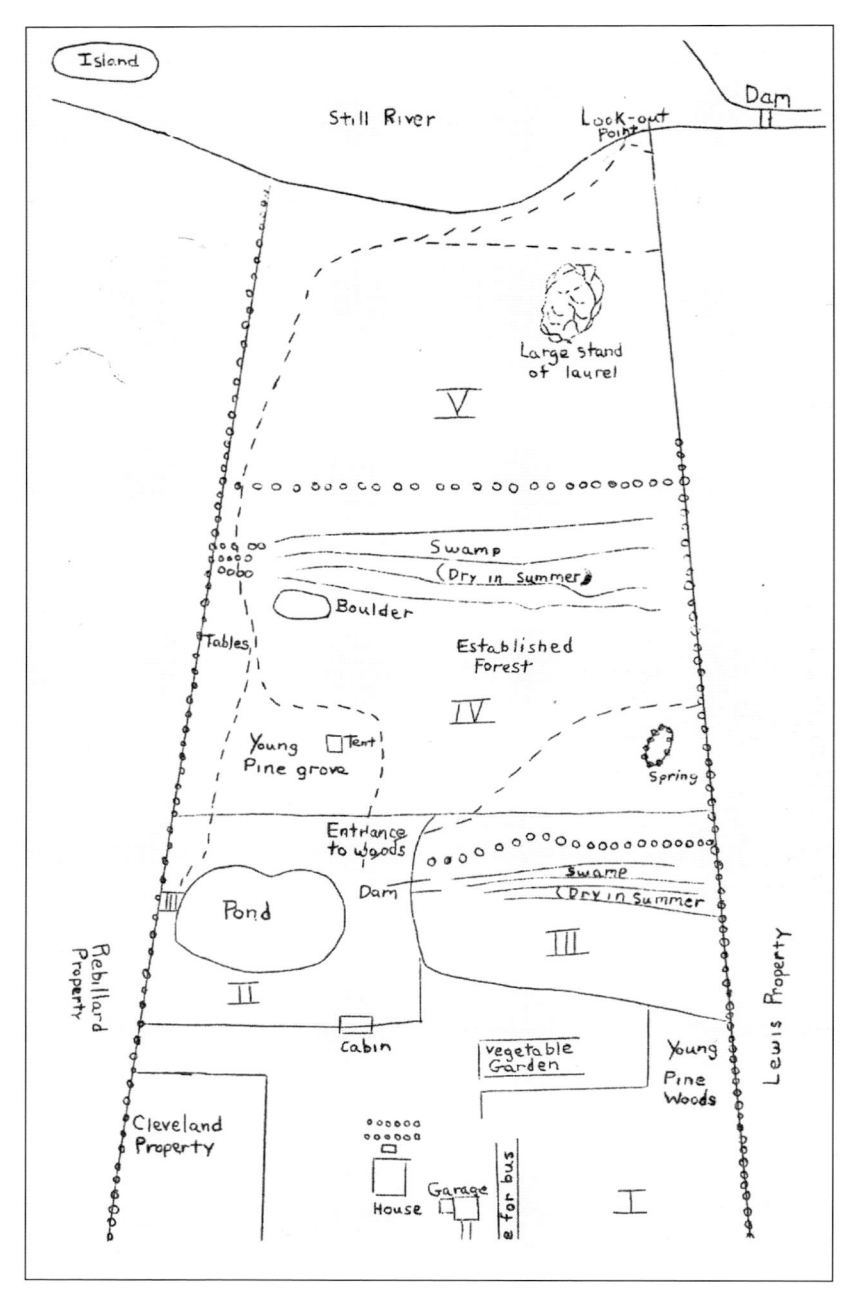

Although this landscape rendering was done in the 1960s, it was true to the gardens designed by author and horticulturalist Ruth Cross. *Charlene LaVoie donation.*

didn't have an apple tree? It is no coincidence that in the book she wrote about her experience in homesteading, she names her husband Adam. During the Depression years, she published her book *Eden on a Country Hill*, which described their adventure, encouraging others to return to the land.

Her love of gardening endeared her to the Winsted Women's Club, and her knowledge of the topic led to a WABC radio program called *Your Garden and Home*. In addition to her book about Edendale, over the next two decades Cross wrote five novels and a nonfiction book, *Wake Up and Garden*.

Just before her husband's death in 1947, she sold Edendale and eventually returned to the South to be near family. She continued to write up until her death in 1981.

LOUIS STONE

Louis Stone, beloved humorist and tall tale teller, began his career with the story of the Winsted Wildman. By his death, he was known worldwide. *Beardsley Library binder.*

Of all the writers who lived in Winsted, no one did more to put Winsted "on the map" than Lou Stone (1875–1933), beloved humorist of all things wild and wonderful in the natural world of his hometown. Stone received his early education from his aunts, the schoolteachers Hattie and Jenny Skinner, in addition to the more formal education at the town's public school.

At the age of thirteen, Lou Stone began work as a printer's devil at the *Winsted Evening Citizen*, a recently organized daily paper started on Main Street near his High Street home. By the time Stone died in 1933, he was the general manager of the newspaper and had brought renown to Winsted and throughout much of the world due to his tall tales of Winsted's animal population. Stone began his claim to fame at the age of nineteen, when due to a shortage of pocket change, he wrote a story about the "Winsted Wild Man" and sent it via wire to other newspapers, as well as the Winsted papers.

This tale was published on August 27, 1895, in the *Winsted Evening Citizen* and also ran again the next day in its sister publication, the *Winsted Herald*—claiming that "a large man, stark naked, and covered with hair all over his body, ran out of a clump of bushes." Over the next few weeks, the increasingly sensationalized story gained steam and attention. Instead of paying Stone, however, the metropolitan newspapers sent their own reporters to try to find this Winsted version of Bigfoot.[293]

The story eventually fizzled out, and the reporters returned to their respective newspapers. But the best was yet to come. Stone now had contacts with the many newspapers, including the nearby *New York World*, *Boston Globe*, *Boston Post* and *Springfield Republican*, among others, as well as the Associated Press, which sent the Winsted byline even farther afield and would eventually reach readers around the world. For more than three decades, Stone sold them short, fanciful stories of the wildlife of Winsted.

An example of Stone's hundreds of animal stories is a favorite horse story:

> *Napoleon, a bay horse who has been drawing a milk wagon here for many years, tired of the tedium of his lot in life and made a break for freedom. But he didn't get far. After dashing down Main street a few blocks, he came to a street crossing just as the traffic light turned red. He stopped from force of habit and Charles Rebillard, his master, came running up and assumed control.*

Stone's specialties were cows and hens—one Winsted cow gave ice cream after his release from an icehouse, and another cow was too shy to let a man milk her unless he donned a dress. Then there was a story about a Plymouth Rock hen that descended from a train when the conductor shouted "Plymouth," as well as the tale about baby chicks raised in a henhouse with a roof so low they developed bowlegs.

Stone's New Year's Day edition continued the saga of Jim, Pete and Dick, the so-called tunneling trout of Winsted. They would visit Stone's Highland Lake cottage; one year, it was reported that they each took a strip of raw liver that Stone gave them from a silver spoon, and then they "gave three fresh-water cheers, got into line, swam in the form of Mr. Stone's three initials backfired once, and sank out of sight."

Newspapers around the country got into the habit of comparing wild stories to those of Winsted or making up stories about the wonders of Winsted. One columnist from the *New York American* claimed, "There are no oysters in Connecticut. Otherwise, Winsted would light up its streets with alternating current from high-powered pearls."

Others wrote poems:

> *A man of ninety danced a jig;*
> *A farmer owns a talking pig;*
> *One has a cow that gives ice cream;*
> *One finds a fortune through a dream;*
> *Ten miles one walks with wooden legs;*
> *A speckled hen lays dated eggs;*
> *A hunter finds a mastodon—*
> *This is the news from Winsted-Conn.*

Stone refused numerous offers from metropolitan newspapers, preferring to stay in his hometown. Others, like the *Chicago Tribune*, opined that if Stone "were permitted to enter the field of imaginative labors and could give freedom to his fancy we might get an American immortal out of Winsted." The *Washington Post*'s response to Winsted's bard: "What a beautiful soul is his! What a rare comfort to tired and practical humanity are his accounts of things he sees! Above all, what a sublimely gorgeous liar! Try as it may, the world can never repay its debt to Winsted."[294]

After Stone's death, Winsted built a bridge with funds from the Works Progress Administration and dedicated it to him. It crossed Sucker Brook.[295]

Chapter 13

DARK DAYS

It is ironic that just as Winsted was heralded "the ideal town," subtle fractures emerged and, sadly, were often ignored that undermined the town's future. The growth of federal regulation to rein in unfair practices, the growth of immigration in the town and the cultural changes it wrought, the plague and its depredations among the working class and two world wars surrounding a deep economic collapse seriously wounded Winsted. There was a bright side, however, as the business leaders began to be less territorial and more willing to work together, which settled a very old problem between West Winsted, the Flats and the east village.

FTC versus Winsted Hosiery

A self-inflicted wound occurred in September 1914 when a complaint of "unfair trade practices in deceptive labeling" against the Winsted Hosiery was filed on the first day of the Federal Trade Commission's (FTC) existence. The hosiery labeled its garments as "Merino," "Worsted" or "Wool" when few of its products were 100 percent wool; indeed, some of the products were 90 percent cotton. The hosiery's attorneys claimed that this was a known practice in the industry and that because the retailers knew that the labels did not accurately list the amount of other materials used in the product, it was the retailers who were being deceptive. The hosiery initially won in Appeals Court, but the case went all the way to the Supreme Court. Justice Louis Brandeis wrote the majority opinion that refuted the claim of the Winsted Hosiery in the case *FTC v. Winsted Hosiery*, decided on April 24, 1922, a cornerstone decision of truth in labeling cases.[296]

Temperance and Immigrants

Much of the workforce, by the twentieth century, was no longer the sons and daughters of farmers but rather those of immigrants. During the building of the town's railroads, the Irish, who had escaped first the intolerance of their British landowners and then the potato famine, found their way to Winsted. Those who feared the "Irish horde" may have privately heaped scorn on them, but since their numbers were still small in comparison to the wider population, they may have been treated with the paternalism of a John Boyd:

> *There is a prevailing tendency to berate the Irish beyond reason. Glaring faults they have, as a result of grinding oppression and cruelty…they have also virtues, which are to be developed only by patience and considerate kindness. They are ignorant, and must be enlightened by education and moral culture.*[297]

In the 1850s and 1860s, small groups of Germans moved into the town of Winchester as Germany's drive toward unification caused some unrest, as did the move away from agriculture to industrialization. Conrad Barreuther of the Kingdom of Wurttenburg, Germany, immigrated to Winsted in 1853 at the age of twenty-two and married the Irish-born Joanna Riordan. In 1867, he brought over a relative, Henry Barreuther. Conrad was naturalized in 1869 and Henry in 1873, an event that Conrad witnessed.

The Kingdom of Wurttenburg was noted for its exports of beer, wine, spirits and pianos. Henry became an organist and a professor of the German language and raised a family of traveling musicians. At first, it was Henry who appeared to be more successful, as his family toured to acclaim and he successfully published both spiritual and secular music. He eventually moved his family to New York City. However, when he died in 1909, he left no will and was virtually penniless.

Conrad Barreuther, farmer and saloonkeeper, immigrated to America in 1853. He often ran into resistance from temperance workers, as did other recent immigrants. *Connecticut Historical Society*.

Conrad, on the other hand, worked as a farmer until 1882, when he incurred the wrath of the town's temperance workers by opening a saloon on Main Street. Temperance workers who had diligently been extolling the evils of drink since 1829 had "spasmodic" success in keeping the town "dry." Nevertheless, in 1872, the state legislature allowed the licensing of taverns, which allowed towns to decide whether they were "wet" or "dry." In licensing liquor establishments, the town would make money in fees. John Boyd in his last years demanded:

> *Where is the board of selectmen who will recommend for license the palatial hotel proprietor and the aboveground saloon-keeper and apothecary, and dare to refuse the subterranean restaurant, be he Yankee, Paddy, or Dutchman?*[298]

As the century came to a close, most of the onus of alcohol consumption was placed on the backs of immigrants. Conrad moved his saloon to Willow Street, but in the latter years of the 1880s, the annual town vote gave victory to the "dry" contingent and Conrad went back to farming. However, increasing numbers of the working class and numbers of immigrants from southern and eastern Europe continued to find their way to Winsted in the 1890s, and the annual vote to license or remain a dry town ended in a victory to the "wets." From 1894 until his death in 1897, Conrad became a saloonkeeper again. His sons, John and Charles, continued the business as Barreuther Brothers.[299]

Their business was attacked by the viciously scurrilous temperance newspaper the *Winsted Sentinel* (1908–11), as were saloons operated by descendants of Irish immigrants like Timothy Canty, who was a bottler of potent potables prior to becoming the saloonkeeper in the Winchester Hotel, and the Bannon brothers, whose sample room near the railroad included various liquors and cigars on Willow Street. The newspaper attacked the saloons, claiming, without evidence, that other businesses and factories were in an economic slump due to the success of the wicked liquor dealers (actually in 1907 there was a financial panic in New York that spread throughout the country that was the larger culprit). And further, the liquor dealers, they proclaimed, were after the morals and health of young boys now that liquor had put the fathers either in jail or in the grave.[300]

When national Prohibition went into effect in 1920, Barreuther Brothers had enough capital to transform its business to an automotive dealership featuring Studebakers and Chevrolet, a business that lasted decades. Meanwhile, the liquor business merely went underground until Prohibition ended, with some brazen enough to sell the illicit product directly across from the police station.[301]

The Great War and the Spanish Flu

In Winsted, essential workers in the factories and their families received the brunt of one of the most deadly pandemics to ever visit itself upon the earth: the misnamed Spanish influenza outbreak—the so-called Spanish flu originated not in Spain but rather, according to some historians and epidemiologists, possibly in Haskell County, Kansas, in January 1918. From there it rapidly spread to a recently built military camp, where new conscripts were trained then sent off to Europe to enter the killing fields of the Great War (World War I). Spain received the blame because it was neutral in the war and reported the outbreaks of this new, virulent disease, while the warring countries clamped down on news coverage. In America,

President Woodrow Wilson encouraged the passage of a sedition act that allowed the government extraordinary powers against those perceived, like newspapers, of hindering the government effort. Therefore, few knew about the virus. The first wave of this pandemic during the spring of 1918 was not particularly lethal, though highly contagious, but the second wave found that the virus had mutated to a virulence not seen since the Black Death in the Middle Ages; Winsted, as the hub of two railroad lines, was not spared.[302]

From reportage in the *Winsted Evening Citizen*, it appears that the first two lives lost were a couple, Mary Oliveri and her husband, Felix, who survived her by a few hours. They were twenty-five years of age and died in the isolation cottage at the Litchfield County Hospital on Spencer Street. Both were first-generation immigrants born in Italy and had lived on Elm Street with their young son. The couple had a double funeral and were buried at the old St. Joseph Cemetery.

Also nearby was the stone for Lewis Colligan, age twenty, who lived on Boyd Street. When the newspaper announced his death on October 9, it mentioned that his brother, Peter, age twenty-five, was also in critical condition. Peter also has a stone in the cemetery, dated 1918.

These residents, along with Mrs. Joseph Haddad, age twenty-six, perished in the first week of October. The staff of doctors was already in short supply in town, as Dr. E.R. Kelsey had recently left to join the troops, where he, too, contracted the disease, though he survived. Dr. D. Reidy

Louis A. Colligan was an early victim of the Spanish influenza outbreak in Winsted. His brother, Peter, also succumbed to the disease. *Author's photograph collection.*

was also among the influenza patients. In addition, the isolation cottage at the Litchfield County Hospital was bursting at the seams with thirty-six patients on October 7. Two days earlier, there had only been nine. The *Winsted Evening Citizen* reported that "every effort is being made to check the spread of the malady. The grammar schools and St. Anthony's school are closed for two weeks or until the danger is past, the theaters are closed until further notice.…St. Anthony's school was fumigated." The Gilbert School was closed the next day. It was also noted that factories "are being operated with greatly depleted working forces and in some instances as many as 30 are out in a single department by reason of sickness." And several of these factories, like the Winsted Hosiery and the New England Knitting Mills, were essential businesses, as they had government contracts for war clothing.

Health officer Dr. S.G. Howd reported on the eighth that Boloslw Polsko, twenty-six, an employee of the Winsted Hosiery Company, died at his home on Main Street. He had only been in the country a year. His funeral was held at St. Joseph's Church, but the location of his grave site could not be determined, as was the case with many of the poor immigrants.

By the ninth, 340 cases of influenza were reported by area physicians. Meanwhile, preparations to open a Red Cross hospital at the Highland Park estate were begun in earnest, as the isolation hospital was overwhelmed. By the next day, three more deaths were reported. Joseph Rizza, forty-five, an employee of the Winsted Edge Tool Company, died. He was a native of Italy and left a wife and daughter. Although it was noted that he was to be buried at Forest View Cemetery, no headstone with his name appears on the headstone inscriptions database listing. Fifteen-year-old Robert Yorker also died that day and was buried in another town, and fourteen-year-old Maxine L. Merrill died at her home at 309 Main Street. She was to have been buried at Forest View Cemetery, but her name does not appear on the WPA database either.

On October 12, Health Officer Howd felt reassured that the epidemic was slowing down, as evidenced by fewer new cases that day, and stated that "people are pretty well awake now to the seriousness of the disease and are taking greater precautions." Gauze masks in public were probably more commonplace, as the instructions for making them had been in the newspaper on the tenth. He estimated that there were four hundred cases in town. Yet the worst was still to come. On the twelfth, it was announced that Peter Colligan, Louis's brother, would be buried the next day. And ten-month-old Genevieve Carrazzo, daughter of Mr. and Mrs. Raffo

Carrazzo, died at her home at 212 Walnut Street. There are no inscriptions on any database for this toddler.

Between the fourteenth and sixteenth, there was an unsettling number of people who succumbed to the disease, including one-year-old Mitchell Maraski, who lived with his parents at 67 Hubbard Street, and eleven-year-old Mildred Hall of Rock Street, who was buried next to Mary Locassio, twenty-six. Hall was a student at the Fourth District School (Mary P. Hinsdale School). Possibly Mary Murray of Spencer Street was a classmate since she was an eleven-year-old who perished two days after Mildred. Dominica Foscana, the six-month-old daughter of Salvo Foscana on Chestnut Street, continued the string of terrible infant and child deaths. Also on Chestnut Street on the seventeenth was Josephine DiCara, who was buried at the old Catholic cemetery. Of all the children who died, the only one with a marker was Mildred Hall; the rest may have had parents too poor to afford a stone, although they may have had wooden or iron crosses at one time to mark the final resting place.

Another heart-wrenching death was that of Helen (Gagnon) Gompert, twenty-two, wife of Frank Gompert. She died on October 14. Her husband, Frank, had enlisted on February 26, 1917, in the U.S. Naval Air Corps stationed in Ireland. They had married on February 18, only eight days prior to his enlistment. It is unlikely they ever saw each other again. Helen was an employee of the New England Knitting Company and was buried at the old St. Joseph Cemetery, not far from her brother-in-law, George Angell, who worked at the New England Pin Company and died exactly one week after Helen.

On October 19, there was a record number of patients at the Red Cross Hospital and the isolation cottage: a total of sixty-four. A plea went out for women or men "accustomed to caring for and nursing the sick." Factories also requested that children between the ages of fourteen and sixteen "who desire to work in factories next week can secure employment certificates." As the ranks of factory workers were thinned by death and the families of the workers, this brought the disease home to their children. And children of all ages continued to die: that very day, fourteen-year-old Mabel Davis on Main Street passed away, and two days earlier, two-year-old Charles Fournier had as well.

By the twenty-first, the numbers of new admissions had fallen, but as often happens, the death toll continued to mount. One very poignant death was that of Dorothy Kremer White, a mother of two who died of the disease while giving birth to her third child, a son, on the twenty-fifth. Also on that day, Sara M. Pfaefflin, twenty-four, an employee of the Seth Thomas Clock Mill in Thomaston, passed away, only eight days after her brother, Thomas, who was employed by the same company.

Originally, the plan was to open the schools on the twenty-fourth, but the continued high rate of deaths kept them closed until November. According to the *Winsted Evening Citizen*, the town clerk's office recorded sixty deaths that month, and fifty-two burial permits had been issued by October 26—most due to the epidemic. A Winsted undertaker said that "he had never seen the time before when money would not open a grave or buy a casket but today, rich and poor alike must wait."

It is likely that deaths from this disease occurred in September prior to anyone realizing that a pandemic had struck the northwest corner and, very likely, more deaths in November, as there were those still in the isolation hospital in critical condition. But news of the end of the war brought reporting of those deaths to a standstill, even though this killer plague brought more death to Winsted than the combined total of both world wars.

Economic Dislocation

The two world wars brought badly needed business to Winsted. Businesses and farming had been in a slump prior to the Great War but picked up as certain businesses received government contracts. However, the short duration of the war left businesses in debt and many workers unemployed. In addition, transportation modes changed due to increased usage of automobiles, taxis and buses. The trolley service was discontinued in 1929, railroad service was severely curtailed and one passenger and freight station was torn down—no longer was Winsted the hub of northwestern Connecticut.

Long-lived businesses began to close their doors. George and Landon Alvord sold their interest in the Empire Knife Company in 1920; the stock was then appraised at $175,000. Six years later, the reorganized company's capitalization had fallen precipitously, and the concern's valuation was a mere $9,500. The stock market crash of 1929 caused the steadily declining company to close its doors in 1930.[303]

One of the oldest and largest of Winsted's companies was the New England Pin Company, which merged with several other pin companies in 1926 and moved to Derby. This was not a complete loss to the town, as the jobs were quickly replaced by the expansion of the New England

Knitting Mills, which purchased the buildings and expanded its already considerable concern.[304]

After the collapse of the country's economy, the Strong Manufacturing Company, maker of silver- and gold-plated coffin fixtures along with other coffin accoutrements, closed its doors. Few could afford or were willing to purchase these luxury items to bury their deceased. The building was purchased in 1937 by Walter Davey and Robert Noble, who formed the Dano Company to manufacture electric coils and transformers, supporting thirty-five to forty employees.[305]

WORLD WAR II

By 1940, the U.S. economy was finally on the upswing. However, on December 7, 1941, the attack on Pearl Harbor once again brought suffering to Americans. All Americans, not just those in the military, were expected to do their part in fighting a two-front war against Japan and Germany, and this extended far beyond just buying war bonds to finance the war.

Americans were expected to do their part in manufacturing the weapons and the necessities of war. A number of Winsted factories became involved in war work. Not surprisingly, the Winsted Hosiery Company and the New England Knitting Mills again received orders for socks and underwear to clothe the troops. This required they discontinue their profitable lines, to the detriment of their bottom line; however, they would have been unable to receive the raw materials required if they had not gone into war work.[306]

Son-Chief Electrics made rubber ponchos for the troops and Pitot tubes that measured air speed and were mounted on the wings of airplanes. For its efforts, the company received the Army-Navy "E" pennant for excellence in quality and quantity of production, and its employees received a pin. Another company that received the reward was the Mason Silk Company. In addition to making thread dyed in appropriate colors for the military, the nylon produced was used in making parachutes. Less than 5 percent of the companies engaged in war work received this recognition.[307]

The Gilbert Clock Company discontinued its clockmaking in Winsted and manufactured fuses and timed detonators in its war work. Yet many Winsted workers were attracted by the much higher pay in other cities.

They took company buses to the Brass Mills of the Naugatuck Valley, while others rode in standing room–only buses to their employment in the aircraft industry around Hartford.[308]

The need to take buses instead of cars was due to enforced rationing of gas, tires and repair parts. Price control and rationing of food, especially sugar and meat, was required to save food for the vast army raised. Citizens were encouraged to grow Victory Gardens on their property to feed themselves and others. Typewriters and shoes were also controlled, and no cars could be built or sold for the duration of the war. Salvage drives for newspapers, nylon stockings, old pots and pans and even cooking fat were recycled for the war effort.[309]

At least 1,413 people from the town of Winchester joined the armed forces, with 30 deaths, including missing in action. Many residents also volunteered for civil defense work as "spotters" for enemy aircraft. In Winsted, the civil defense hut was built on top of the Soldiers' Monument, and volunteers manned the facility day and night.[310]

At the conclusion of the war, the pent-up demand for consumer products did not explode until some years after the war, as there was a glut of military supplies on hand; in particular, there was a desire for clothing made from the new synthetics instead of the wool/cotton blends produced in the Winsted factories. In addition, returning veterans were guaranteed employment, thus putting others, in those jobs, out of work.[311]

East–West Divide Ends

However, not all was doom and gloom in the first half of the twentieth century. Winsted business owners—whether in West Winsted, the Flats or the east village—began to see their bickering as pointless. Prior to 1910, there were two social clubs known as Clifton and Winchester whose business members belonged to two different sections of town. By 1910, leaders in the business community who belonged to the Winsted Business Men's Association realized that it would be good for business and the town if the two social clubs merged. Property was purchased, a clubhouse was built in 1911 on Wheeler Street and the Winsted Club was opened as a social gathering place for businessmen and other prominent men in the community. In 1914, the Winsted Business Men's Association merged with the Winsted Chamber of Commerce.[312]

The merging of the eastern sector with the western portion of the town finally ended the longest and most bizarre argument within the business community: where should the post office be located? In the early years of the town, the argument was where to put the houses of worship. Sometimes it would take years to come to a compromise, but this was nothing compared to the post office fiasco, which lasted 135 years! Starting in 1802, until the federal government built the central post office in the midst of the Great Depression in 1937, there was a running feud as to which side of town should have the benefit of the post office.

At first, it appeared that the problem was the patronage system, as when a Democrat was appointed to the position of postmaster in the east village in 1802. In 1806, Solomon Rockwell wrote to the postmaster general on behalf of the businessmen in West Winsted asking that the post office be moved to the opposite side of town, a little more than a mile away. In 1807, Federalist Horace Higley, whose tavern was the site of the early town meetings, became the postmaster. The post office remained in the tavern in West Winsted for about forty years under various postmasters, including William S. Holabird and John Boyd.[313]

Amy Jones was employed by the federal government to paint the mural *Lincoln's Arbiter Settles the Winsted Post Office Controversy*, which depicts the endless debate about the location of the post office. *Author's photograph collection.*

It is not clear when the battle became more heated, possibly in the late 1840s, when the post office moved to the east, back to the west and then back to the east village in a little more than a year. One way to settle the problem was to locate the post office on the Flats in the middle of the town. Unfortunately, that made both east and west howl with rage. The compromise that held for decades was two post offices, starting in about 1849 when Gideon Hall became postmaster in a building on his property south of the town green, while George Dudley operated the West Winsted Post Office near or in the Beardsley House hotel.[314]

Still, that would not be the end of the tale. In 1898, the assistant postmaster general decided to step in and create a *third* post office on Main Street—a street that was not even two miles long. He ordained that the post office in West Winsted would be Station A, a post office near North Main would be Station B and the Main Street post office would adjoin the Opera House block on the Flats.[315]

The current post office at 328 Main Street was built with federal funds under the direction of an appointed commission and the Winsted Chamber of Commerce. The Treasury Department employed artist Amy Jones of Saranac, New York, to paint a mural on the interior west wall. The oil-on-canvas painting entitled *Lincoln's Arbiter Settles the Winsted Post Office Controversy* depicts the arguing of the businessmen about the location of the post office. Why Lincoln? According to legend, President Abraham Lincoln was thought to have said, "The fight over the location of the Winsted Post Office has given me more trouble than the whole Civil War."[316]

THE CORNELIO LEGACY

The building of the trolley from Torrington to Winsted in 1897 brought to town many hardworking Italians who worked on the line. This "Italian horde" stayed, with many moving to Chestnut Street—not far from the Catholic church in an area that would become known as Little Italy. In 1903, the family of Santo Cornelio was one of a number of families who emigrated from Floridia, Sicily, to Winsted.

One of Santo's sons, Carmine, became a very successful automobile dealer in Litchfield County. A descendant of Carmine described him as a "civic-minded person who loved his adopted homeland, but who never forgot the land of his birth." As his business boomed due to pent-up demand at the conclusion of World War II, he parlayed some of his earnings in 1948 into production of a film of Winsted, his adopted hometown, to bring to his homeland so that they could "once again see the faces of their relatives, and also to show them the successful life of the 'American Dream.'"[317]

The film was produced by professionals and filmed in color. The camera was probably mounted on the hood of Carmine's powder-blue 1948 Oldsmobile convertible. Vignettes of Italian life in America included visits with the various Italian American–owned groceries, liquor stores and barbershops, as well as festivals and picnics. But it is the drive down Main Street itself that lingers in the hearts and minds of all those who view the film. Seven years later, it would all be gone.

Chapter 14

DELUGE!

Their names were Connie and Diane. Formerly hurricanes, as tropical storms they did not directly hit Connecticut, but their energy in moisture-laden air produced prodigious rainfall that destroyed Winsted and many communities that, like Winsted, had built up alongside swift rivers to support their need for water to power their factories.

Connie formed in the eastern Atlantic on August 3, 1955, and by the next day had reached hurricane status. After it passed by Puerto Rico, it quickly became a Category 4 hurricane on the Saffir-Simpson scale. Soon after, it headed northward, losing steam, and plowed into North Carolina. From there it moved northwest into the Chesapeake Bay area and was absorbed by a front over Lake Huron. The rain, however, covered much of New England. The storm dropped four to six inches of rain, which alleviated a severe drought that had caused widespread complaints in Winsted from factory owners who could not get enough water power and from residents who complained of the stench from the Mad River.[318]

Diane formed on August 7 and followed a similar path as Connie, although it was a less powerful hurricane, only climbing to a Category 2. By the time it came ashore (also in North Carolina), it was "merely" a tropical storm. It then changed trajectory, exited New Jersey and ran eastward over the warm waters of the Long Island Sound. All of the Northeast received torrential rain, but Connecticut was the most severely damaged. In a twenty-four-hour period, the rainfall reached almost seventeen inches in a station just outside Winsted.[319]

Winsted had a significant history of floods. Presumably before the so-called Jefferson Flood of 1801, flooding occurred whenever the Housatonic, Naugatuck or particularly the Connecticut River flooded. Most historically recorded flooding after 1801 appears to fulfill those benchmarks, which suggests that there were five significant floods dating back to the horrific flood of 1635, which almost ended Connecticut settlement. During the cleanup of the August flood of 1955, a member of the Army Corps of Engineers said that he found evidence of a catastrophic flood nine hundred years prior![320]

Frank DeMars mentioned the flood of 1853 in these terms: "One of Winsted's periodic floods visited the village early in May....The Still River bridge was washed away and no mail was received in town from Saturday until Thursday." This was a major flood in New England, and the Connecticut River at Hartford rose almost twenty-nine feet. In October 1869, a flood occurred in October, produced by a hurricane that the *Winsted Herald* stated was "the greatest, wettest, most widespread and most disastrous storm... since the days of Columbus and Vespucci." A late-season hurricane in 1927 caused the Connecticut River to rise twenty-nine feet, and although Winsted lost no bridges, the retail sector was harmed and Winsted was isolated due to floodwaters surrounding the town.[321]

Not all floods were caused by hurricanes. March 12–18, 1936, saw a flood due to heavy rains, melting snow and ice jams. The Connecticut River had its worst flood ever, with water levels reaching almost thirty-eight feet over flood stage. In nearby New Hartford, the Greenwoods Dam collapsed under the strain and swept away three bridges, many homes and buildings. Winsted, in its generosity (and gratitude for being spared from the brunt of the storm), took up collections of money and food for its neighbors. Winsted had saved itself as town workers diverted water from Rugg Brook to Crystal Lake and then to Highland Lake, which "relieved the situation on Mad River for several hours," so when the inevitable happened and Highland Lake flooded, the Mad River was no longer at its highest point and the worst danger had passed. The *Winsted Evening Citizen* announced, "Fishing Good on Main Street," as fish were washed onto the road.[322]

The Great New England Hurricane of 1938 created widespread destruction throughout New England due to winds and tidal waves in conjunction with a frontal system that preceded it that brought ten to seventeen inches of rain to the region. Although northwest Connecticut was not the hardest hit, it was still the worst flooding most residents had seen to date. In Winsted, swirling waters carried dangerous flotsam, autos and even

The flood of 1938 was four feet deep with a rapid current, but few buildings were destroyed. The Winsted Motor Sales survived, only to be destroyed in 1955. *Mike and Sherry Connell donation.*

a home that was swept away. Main Street was under four feet of water with a wicked current, which made rescue dangerous and difficult. Little did they know that this was just a "dry" run for a "thousand-year" flood that would strike the community in seventeen years.[323]

The New Year's Eve flood from December 31, 1948, to January 1, 1949, was triggered by rain on frozen ground. The damage was inconvenient but minimal due to low levels of water at Highland Lake and the new reservoirs in Nepaug and Barkhamsted. The "heavy dew" did leave about five feet of water on Main Street and disrupt rail service while flooding cellars. The persistent flooding in Winsted brought the Army Corps of Engineers to survey the damage and warn the town that projected federal aid, originally offered in 1946 to dig the trench for the Mad River deeper and line the trench with stone, was in danger of being diverted due to inaction from local officials. Mayor P. Francis Hicks of Winsted was able to get this through the town's board and the work was completed, but the deepened trench was no match for the events of August 1955.

During the flood of 1938, horrified tenants watched the rapid, swirling floodwaters. *Mike and Sherry Connell donation.*

On August 9, 1955, ten days prior to Winsted's "Black Friday," the *Winsted Evening Citizen* reported, "Highland Lake Level Being Watched Closely." George S. Light, president of the Union Pin Company, had control of the gate at Highland Lake and closely monitored the water level of the lake. Due to the persistent drought, the water level was thirty-two inches below overflow. Therefore, he only opened the gate for a short time each day to provide water power to the factories below and to keep the river bed clean and free of odor. Less than a week later, the precipitation from Connie relieved the stress produced by the dry summer.

Sporadic rain occurred throughout the next few days as remnants of Connie left the area and Diane approached on August 18. However, there was a brief clearing at 5:00 p.m. on the eighteenth. Many youngsters and their families attended the latest Disney film, *Lady and the Tramp*, playing at the Strand Theater, but found heavy rainfall as they left the theater. At 11:25 p.m., WTIC radio erroneously forecast "occasional showers."[324]

While people slept, many millions of gallons of rain poured down on the hills of northwest Connecticut. "Winsted," as Pulitzer Prize winner John

Hersey wrote, "lies in an irregular bowl formed by the steep slopes of Street Hill, Platt Hill, Ward's Hill, Second Cobble, and several lesser hills." He noted that "at one time Highland Lake turned the wheels of eleven factories scattered down the ravine, which drops a hundred and fifty feet in its half-mile course before it joins the Mad River in Winsted's west end."[325]

At Highland Lake, teenager Ted Zoli and his friend spent the night at Ted's parents' house, fortunately located on a hill, due to the wind and pouring rain. They tied the friend's boat to wooden lawn furniture and an oak tree in the middle of the Zoli's property. In the morning, they found the lake had covered over the boat and furniture, and a neighbor had to leave her home and was sleeping on the Zoli's couch. All that was visible of the neighbor's house that morning was the peak. The lake was many feet over flood stage, fed directly by rain and the flooding of Crystal Lake, Rugg Brook and the various brooks and streams feeding into the lake.[326]

Later, the boys found near the spillways, the last line of defense from the lake's power, that water approximately five feet deep was raging over the spillways and had pushed cars into the spillway overflow. The Union Pin Company was heavily damaged, and the nearby knife company, including the ground it stood on, was washed away, as were hundreds of new appliances as the water raged through the Winsted Hardware Company.

The water continued its advance on the defenseless city below, although it did detour onto Meadow Street, destroying the new addition of Son-Chief Electric and flooding the homes along the lovely, scenic neighborhood that ran parallel to Main Street.

In Winsted, sirens went off at 1:15 a.m., alerting the city of danger. An hour later, the power went out. Civil defense workers were busy warning occupants to go to high ground, but due to the rabbit warren of old wooden buildings, with their shared fire escapes and porches, some doors were overlooked, trapping residents. It is unlikely that many living on Main Street were unaware of the dire emergency by then, as buildings began to twist and contort on their foundations as water began running through the ground floors.[327]

By daybreak, those on higher ground near the railroad station and on the high ground of St. Joseph's Church were horrified to see that water, sixteen feet deep in some places, especially near the Flats, appeared to reach the canopies over the store windows. They could not believe their eyes that the current, traveling an estimated thirty to fifty miles per hour, was sweeping before it everything in its path. Buicks from Winsted Motor Sales dove and bobbed like breaching whales; the back seat of one car was draped over

Tenements along the Mad River in West Winsted. In the eastern portion, tenements were much more crowded with stairways and had, as the story goes, latrines hanging over the river. *Connecticut Historical Society.*

utility wires. The roof of Winsted Motor, which had been located across from the YMCA, was deposited in front of town hall, and a car from that company was smashed against the building where numerous police and civil defense workers were trapped. Manchester Feed and Grain was destroyed, as was Isaacson's Store on the opposite corner of Elm and Main Streets across from the Winchester Hotel. Demolition occurred as the rear was washed out and caused the roof to cave. The four-story Clifton Hotel drifted down Main Street and came to rest in the old ballfield, with its two bottom floors scored away on the trip. The Central Hotel, on the opposite side of the road from the Hotel Winchester, in the very heart of downtown Winsted, came unmoored but was kept from traveling by the nearby utility pole, which stopped its path on the corner of Bridge Street. That steel bridge was one of the ten bridges lost that night. On the north side of the river, along Main Street next to the bridge, three tenements twisted and fell. What wasn't destroyed by the raging river was demolished by the battering debris accumulating in the swiftly moving current.

The Still River, which merged with the Mad River near the town Green, belied its name. It also looked for prey, destroying a church, washing out the bridge near the Winsted Hosiery, flooding homes and causing hundreds of thousands of dollars of damage to what had been the largest employer in town, the William L. Gilbert Clock Company.[328]

The small mom and pop stores lost their inventory of clothing, food and fixtures. Taxicabs and hairdresser chairs caught in the current were remarked on. Few shop windows remained in place, and when the water disappeared two days later, almost as distressing was what had been uncovered. The infrastructure of the town was gone—sidewalks and blacktop tossed about, and broken sewer, gas and water mains were exposed in a canyon that had been gouged eight feet deep. Winsted looked like it had been aerial bombed.

By 3:00 p.m., helicopters began to arrive at the Central School on Wetmore Avenue, as did National Guard units. Water and food were top priorities and were there quickly. The grim task of locating the dead, governing, tallying the cost and starting the plans for recovery were begun. The victims included the following:

Neither Connie nor Diane were hurricanes, nor did they directly hit Connecticut, but the rainfall produced twelve- to sixteen-foot-deep raging currents that destroyed Winsted's industrial center in 1955. *Author's photograph collection.*

John Gould, twenty-eight, from Highland Lake and reported missing, had volunteered to knock on doors and tell people on the river side of Main Street to leave their homes. His remains were found several days later.

The Clifton Hotel yielded the body of Sinclair Meggison, fifty-two. Meggison, who had been staying at the hotel, had encouraged other guests to depart before the water had come up. For some unexplained reason, he decided to spend the night. Three days later, his body was found.

Concettena Zappula, sixty-five, refused to leave her home near the Still River. Floodwaters washed her off the roof in the darkness.

Maney Leshay, seventy-three, who sold newspapers and cigars in his store on the first floor of the Winchester Hotel, was driving down Holabird Avenue on his way to work, not aware that it was not water covering the bridge near the Winsted Hosiery, but rather that the bridge was no longer there. His body was found downstream, still strapped in his car.

Mary Machrone, forty-four, drowned when a rescue boat hit a bridge and capsized.

Josephine Cornelio, forty-nine, and her brother Sebastian were stranded in their tenement. Several attempts to reach them failed. Eventually, the rescue was made, but Josephine panicked and capsized the boat. The rescuers were able to save Josephine's brother and themselves but were unable to rescue the fearful woman. Her body was found several days later in an inaccessible field of debris and had to be removed via helicopter. This recent arrival from Floridia, Sicily, was undoubtedly part of the extended Cornelio family who had recorded the 1948 film of Winsted, the last visible record of Winsted prior to the flood.

William Samele, fifty-seven, a bartender, was watching the attempted rescue of Josephine Cornelio when his apartment house washed away.

Two of the flood's victims had been swept into the basement of the Gilbert Clock Company, according to "The Disaster Bulletin #1," released Saturday, August 20, and issued by John M. Slocum, Winsted resident and staff reporter for the *Hartford Times*. No newspapers were able to get into Winsted, and the town's newspaper, the *Winsted Evening Citizen*, was damaged. Mayor P. Francis Hicks used this bulletin to apprise citizens that the town was under martial law and that no one was allowed on Main Street after dark, which was enforced by National Guardsman to prevent looting. The town health officer, Dr. Francis Gallo, announced that as soon as a vaccine was received to prevent typhoid all residents would be inoculated. Residents north of the river would receive their injections at the Central School and those south of the river at Holland Beach at Highland Lake.

The dedication stone for victims of the 1955 flood has been erected on the Winsted town Green. *Author's photograph collection.*

Bulletin #2 Sunday (misdated as Sunday, August 20, 1955)
It is estimated that 1,500 are homeless and that many buildings on Main
St. will have to come down. The persons who will make the decision, it is
said, will be efficient Army engineers.

Bulletin #4 (Tuesday, Aug. 23, 1955)
A quick assessment of the damage in Bulletin #4 distributed on Tuesday,
August 23 revealed these approximate costs of damage:
Residential: $3,000,000
Industrial: 11,000,000
Commercial: 13,500,000
Private owned: 370,000

The total of $27,870,000 did not include publicly owned utilities, roads and more. The total in 1955 dollars was expected to be in the vicinity of $50 million.

Work was begun quickly, but it would take five years to complete the repairs needed by the city. Of 200 businesses affected, at least 170 did not return. Of the 25 factories, all but one, the New England Knitting Mill, returned. This large employer, located on Main and Bridge Streets, had actually ceased to operate in 1954 until its large inventory was sold. The massive destruction to its primary building along Main Street informed its decision to close permanently.[329]

It was decided that on the river side of Main Street, between the area across from Chestnut Street down to Division Street along the river, buildings (whether repairable or not) were to be removed to serve the state's decision to widen the highway, aided by members of the Winsted Industrial Foundation, who organized in 1943. They comprised former officers of the William F. Gilbert Clock Company, who accepted subscriptions, primarily from other manufacturing concerns, whose goal was to tear down "unsightly" buildings located on the river side of Main Street. They then sold the land along the river to the Connecticut Highway Department. The money received from the purchase was donated to the Winsted Hospital and the YMCA.[330]

The 1958 Congressional hearings for Public Works Appropriations included a discussion from those on the East Coast who had been damaged by the 1955 natural disasters. Winsted addressed the need for a dry dam to protect the town and the Farmington Valley watershed. By incorporating the needs of other communities, the Town of Winchester hoped to avoid paying a portion of the dam. Backing the plea for a flood prevention dam paid for by the federal government was a letter from Hadleigh H. Howd of the Sterling Name Tape Company, who was chosen to administer Small Business Administration (SBA) loans to homeowners and manufacturers. He stated that "there was acute suffering and extreme damage to property and the borrowers will be indebted for years to come." He also warned that

> *the William L. Gilbert Clock Corp., the town's largest industry employing approximately 400 people, received a disaster loan from the Treasury Department of the United States in the amount of $606,100. This loan is secured by a mortgage on the entire real estate, plant and equipment. The flood in this instance caused loss of operations, loss of machinery, equipment and inventory and other damage which ran into hundreds of thousands of dollars with the result that the company is in very poor financial condition at the present time.[331]*

Throughout the twentieth century, the clock company had flirted with financial disaster and was sent into receivership in 1932. In 1934, the company was re-formed into the William L. Gilbert Clock Corporation. By 1954, it was seeing modest profits, but the flood put an end to any chance of profitability. It was purchased by General Computing Machines Corporation to produce adding machines and clocks. Still, it remained unprofitable and was closed in December 1964. It was the last victim of the Flood of '55.

Although the people of the town of Winchester may not have understood it at first, the challenge they now faced would not merely be corrected by burning debris, repairing, rebuilding and repaving—these would be new challenges that old mill towns in the last few decades had faced. The town needed to reimagine a new economy and a new society built on the great bones of the town's past. It is a work in progress.

NOTES

Chapter 1

1. The Saybrook Fort incident of 1675 is summarized from these sources: Albert E. Van Dusen, *Connecticut* (New York: Random House, 1973), 82–83; Elias B. Sanford, *A History of Connecticut* (Boston: Rand Avery Company, 1887), 80–82; William Henry Gocher, *Wadworth, Or the Charter Oak* (Hartford, CT: W.H. Gocher, 1904), 265–67; J.H. Trumbull ed., *The Public Records of the Colony of Connecticut*, 3 vols. (Hartford, CT: F.A. Brown, 1852), vol. 2, 569–74; George Bancroft, *History of the Colonization of the United States*, vol. 2 (Boston: Charles C. Little and James Brown, 1841), 58; Benjamin Trumbull, DD, *A Complete History of Connecticut*, vol. 1 (Hartford, CT: Hudson & Goodwin, 1797), 343–46.
2. Sanford, *History of Connecticut*, 75–77; Van Dusen, *Connecticut*, 23, 67–70.
3. Sanford, *History of Connecticut*, 89.
4. Ibid., 81.
5. Ibid., 81–82.
6. Trumbull, *Public Records of the Colony of Connecticut*, vol. 3, 225.
7. Ibid., "Petition to the King, August 24, 1686," 370–71.
8. Ibid., "Letter from Edward Randolph to Governor Treat and Council," 370–72.
9. Ibid., 376.
10. Gocher, *Wadworth, Or the Charter Oak*, 306–54. Joseph Wadsworth's colorful, and meandering, account of the Charter Oak incident includes

his participation in the hiding—and retrieval—of Connecticut's charter. See Sanford, *History of Connecticut*, 94–96, with his important footnote on the duplicate charter; Van Dusen, *Connecticut*, 97–98.

11. Trumbull, *Public Records of the Colony of Connecticut*, vol. 3, 388–91; Sanford, *History of Connecticut*, 95.

12. Sanford, *History of Connecticut*, 97–98.

13. Gocher, *Wadworth, Or the Charter Oak*, 350–54.

14. Sanford, *History of Connecticut*, 96f; *Winsted Herald*, February 18, 1903, 1; *Committee on Historical Publications: The Charter of Connecticut, 1662* (New Haven, CT: Yale University Press, 1933), 1–8. There is a very good argument to be made that there is no such thing as an "original" or a "duplicate" charter. Both are written the same day, both have the seal and both are the law. Duplicates were made during the days of hazardous ocean travel so that they could be sent on separate ships. If there is an "original," it is in the patent office in London. At least that copy did not fall to the indignity of being used to stiffen a lady's bonnet!

Chapter 2

15. Charles J. Hoadley, ed., *The Public Records of the Colony of Connecticut*, (Hartford, CT: Case, Lockwood and Brainard Company, 1872), vol. 6, 127.

16. Ibid., 341–48.

17. Ibid., 403–4; Trumbull, *Complete History of Connecticut*, vol. 2, 98.

18. Hoadley, *Public Records of the Colony of Connecticut*, vol. 7, 44.

19. John Boyd, *Annals and Family Records of Winchester, Conn.* (Hartford, CT: Case, Lockwood & Brainard, 1873), 14.

20. John J. O'Brien, *Winchester: Beginning of a Town and a Nation* (Winsted, CT: Winchester Press, 1976), 4–6.

21. Boyd, *Annals and Family Records*, 32–33.

22. Ibid., 33–34.

23. Ibid., 32, 40.

24. O'Brien, *Winchester*, 9–10.

25. Ibid., 23–29.

26. Boyd, *Annals and Family Records*, 27–29.

27. Ibid., 266–67.

28. Ibid., 29; O'Brien, *Winchester*, 22. O'Brien thought that Balcom had moved out of Connecticut after 1808; however, Balcom died in Winsted in that year. His probated will can be found online on Ancestry.com

under Connecticut, Wills and Probated Records, 1609–1999, Hartford Probate Packets, Norfolk Probate District, Estate of Balcom, John, Winchester, 1808.

29. O'Brien, *Winchester*, 11–12.

30. Benjamin F. Hubbell, "The New England Combination Gun, 1730–1775," *American Society of Arms Collectors*, no. 8 (Fall 1963): 8–10.

31. Boyd, *Annals and Family Records*, 44–45.

32. Ibid., 45–46; O'Brien, *Winchester*, 133.

33. O'Brien, *Winchester*, 133; Boyd, *Annals and Family Records*, 164; Reverend A.G. Hibbard, *History of the Town of Goshen, Connecticut* (Hartford, CT: Case, Lockwood & Brainard, 1897), 171, 371.

34. Boyd, *Annals and Family Records*, 45–46.

35. Ibid., 75–79; Hoadley, *Public Records of the Colony of Connecticut*, vol. 13, 42.

36. Boyd, *Annals and Family Records*, 81–85; Hoadley, *Public Records of the Colony of Connecticut*, vol. 13, 500.

37. Boyd, *Annals and Family Records*, 44–45.

38. Ibid., 43–44.

Chapter 3

39. Richard Buel Jr., *Dear Liberty: Connecticut's Mobilization for the Revolutionary War* (New York: Columbia University Press, 1980), 15–16.

40. Ibid., 19.

41. Ibid., 26.

42. Hoadley, *Public Records of the Colony of Connecticut*, vol. 14, 83–90.

43. Boyd, *Annals and Family Records*, 161.

44. Henry P. Johnston, *Record of Service Men in the I. War of the Revolution…II. War of 1812…III. Mexican War* (Hartford, CT: Case Lockwood & Brainard Company, 1880), 17, 19.

45. Willard Sterne Randall, *Benedict Arnold: Patriot and Traitor* (New York: William Morrow, 1990), 86–89; James L. Nelson, *Benedict Arnold's Navy: The Ragtag Fleet that Lost the Battle of Lake Champlain but Won the American Revolution* (Camden, ME: McGraw Hill Professional, 2006), 15.

46. Randall, *Benedict Arnold*, 98; Nelson, *Benedict Arnold's Navy*, 68, 128–29.

47. Hibbard, *History of the Town of Goshen*, 119; O'Brien, *Winchester*, 119–20; American Wars, "Connecticut Continental Troops, Fourth Regiment—Colonel Benjamin Hinman, 1775," http://www.americanwars.org/ct-american-revolution/connecticut-continental-troops-fourth-regiment-1775.

48. Johnston, *Record of Service Men*, 79, 81–82, 84.

49. Ibid., 93.

50. David McCullough, *1776: Illustrated Edition* (New York: Simon & Schuster, 2009), 69–101.

51. Hoadley, *Public Records of the Colony of Connecticut*, vol. 15, 415–16.

52. McCullough, *1776*, 130.

53. Ibid., 185–90.

54. Payne Kenyon Kilbourne, *Sketches and Chronicles of the Town of Litchfield, Connecticut* (Hartford, CT: Case, Lockwood and Company, 1859), 96–101; Johnston, *Record of Service Men*, 84, 423.

55. Shelton church records.

56. O'Brien, *Winchester*, 120, 129, 135.

57. McCullough, *1776*, 104–5.

58. Ibid., 209–10.

59. Ibid., 222.

60. Buel, *Dear Liberty*, 81–82.

61. Ibid., 82.

62. Ibid., 100.

63. Ibid., 92–93.

64. Ibid., 116–17.

65. Ibid., 111–16.

66. Ibid., 111–18; O'Brien, *Winchester*, 114; Johnston, *Record of Service*, 438, 493; Hibbard, *History of Goshen*, 138.

67. O'Brien, *Winchester*, 117, 139, 151, 153, 169. O'Brien is incorrect on several facts regarding Judah Roberts, who did replace his father, who was ill and died several years later. Judah was not twelve, but rather two weeks shy of his fifteenth birthday. His brother Samuel was fifteen when he enlisted. Although they were probably the youngest to sign up for service in the Revolution from the town of Winchester, this was not uncommon. Children as young as nine went with their fathers into battle. See Caroline Cox's *Boy Soldiers of the American Revolution* (2016). Judah Roberts is not mentioned in George Washington's memoirs, nor in the Cox book. The memoir is online.

68. O'Brien, *Winchester*, 105.

69. Bob Griggs, "The Facts About Buried Hessian Soldiers in Colebrook," Colebrook Historical Society website, www.colebrookhistoricalsociety.org.

70. August Wilhelm Du Roi, *Journal of Du Roi the Elder, Lieutenant and Adjutant, in the Service of the Duke of Brunswick, 1776–1778* (New York: D. Appleton & Company, Agents, 1911), 135. This was translated from the original

German manuscript in the Library of Congress, Washington, D.C., by Charlotte S.J. Epping.

71. Valley Forge Legacy, www.valleyforgemusterroll.org. This is a handy but possibly incomplete roll. When checked originally, Samuel Roberts was discharged in January with the other two men. Now he doesn't appear on the list at all. Possibly he was discharged immediately upon going into quarters due to his young age. He continued to serve throughout the war in various companies until at least 1782.

72. O'Brien, *Winchester*, 100, 148, 149.

73. Ibid., 127, 157.

74. Boyd, *Annals and Family Records.*

Chapter 4

75. O'Brien, *Winchester*, 89.

76. Boyd, *Annals and Family Records*, 223–24.

77. Van Dusen, *Connecticut*, 191.

78. Albert Laverne Olson, *Agricultural Economy and the Population in Eighteenth Century Connecticut*, Connecticut Tercentenary pamphlet no. 40 (New Haven, CT: Yale University Press, 1935), 25.

79. Boyd, *Annals and Family Records*, 48.

80. Oneida Indian Nation Timeline, 1788, www.oneidanation.com.

81. Elliott B. Bronson, *A New England Village Green: A Paper Delivered before the Winchester Historical Society, Winsted, Connecticut, October Thirteen, Nineteen Hundred and Thirteen by Elliott B. Bronson, President*, 1914 (revised 1971). This paper can be accessed at the Beardsley Library genealogy room. This hypothesis was, in short, ridiculous. The vote happened twelve years before Seth Hills set out for Oneida territory. And why would Reverend Publius Booge be upset enough to give his notice since he was hired as a minister years after the vote in 1785? Booge never became the minister in Vernon Center, but rather accepted a position in Vermont. Very strange indeed. I checked all the names on the Baschard Patent—only nineteen of the thirty-eight could remotely be charged to Winchester. Many were married to daughters and granddaughters of the Hills. Many of the remaining were from Torrington and western Massachusetts.

82. Find A Grave, www.findagrave.com. Publius Virgilius Booge (also spelled "Bogue") mentions the problem with the evangelist Charles Grandison

Finney. Booge's brother, also a preacher, was driven out of his profession by the popular evangelist as well.

83. Boyd, *Annals and Family Records*, 223.

84. Ibid., 43, 45; Van Dusen, *Connecticut*, 194–95.

85. Van Dusen, *Connecticut*, 195.

86. Boyd, *Annals and Family Records*, 41, 158–59.

87. Ibid., 186; Filley/Philley Family File Beardsley Library.

88. Boyd, *Annals and Family Records*, 41, 186; Filley/Philley Family File Beardsley Library (see notes from Roger E. Filley and Jane Philley Robertson). Although I can't prove it, most of the information that Boyd is probably using about those who emigrated comes from the son of the Seth Hills family Deacon Ira Hills of Vernon, New York, according to Boyd. I tend to treat that information with a great deal of skepticism since much of it has proven to be incorrect.

89. Eliphaz Alvord, *Connecticut Towns: Winchester-Winsted in 1813* (Hartford, CT: Acorn Club of Connecticut, 1961), 6.

90. *Winsted Journal*, December 31, 1981, 2.

Chapter 5

91. Alvord, *Connecticut Towns*, 3, 5.

92. Ibid., 7.

93. Ibid., 6, 7.

94. Ibid., 7.

95. Ibid., 4.

96. Ibid.,.

97. Ibid., 10.

98. Ibid., 13–14.

99. Frank H. DeMars and Elliott P. Bronson, *Winsted and the Town of Winchester* (Dublin: Parkgate Printing Works, 1972), 244.

100. Ibid., 245.

101. Ibid., 5.

102. Ibid., 245–46, 248.

103. Ibid., 255; "Illustrated Catalogue Wm. Gilbert Clock Co.," 179, excerpt found in William L. Gilbert Family File, Beardsley Library.

104. "Illustrated Catalogue Wm. Gilbert Clock Co.," 179.

105. Bob Griggs, "Riley Whiting and the Local Clock Industry," Whiting Family File, Beardsley Library.

106. "Illustrated Catalogue Wm. Gilbert Clock Co.," 180.

107. DeMars and Bronson, *Winsted and the Town of Winchester*, 252.

108. Ibid., 252–53.

109. O'Brien, *Winchester*, 70.

110. Ibid., 64, 70.

111. Bronson, *New England Village Green*, 3.

112. Ibid., 4; Anna K. Gale, *Colonial Winchester* (Winsted, CT: Dowd Printing Company, 1971), 8.

113. Bronson, *New England Village Green*, 5–6.

114. Ibid., 14–16.

115. Ibid., 18.

116. Gale, *Colonial Winchester*, 9–10.

117. Ibid., 11.

118. Virginia Shultz-Charette, "Town of Winchester: Brief History of the Education, Structure, Financing and Redistricting of the Town's Schools, 1773–1960, Part I—Public Schools," *Winsted Journal*, February 20, 2015, 1.

119. Ibid.

120. District School Map, 1874, Beardsley Library, Genealogy room.

121. Virginia Shultz-Charette, "Town of Winchester…Brief History of the Education Structure, Financing and Redistricting of the Town's Schools, 1773–1960, Part II—Private Schools," *Winsted Journal*, March 27, 2015, 1.

122. Ibid.

123. Boyd, *Annals and Family Records*, 431.

Chapter 6

124. Ibid., 97.

125. Ibid.

126. Ibid., 99; *Hartford Daily Courant*, "The Farm and the Garden," December 13, 1854, page 2, mentions the Hurlbut apple; T.S. Gold on behalf of the Connecticut Agricultural Society, "Biographical Sketch of Lemuel Hurlbut," *Hartford Daily Courant*, July 8, 1856. These last two articles can be accessed through the Connecticut State Library's Historical Newspapers site.

127. Judge George Carrington's handwritten lecture notes, 12, Hurlbut Family Files, Beardsley Library.

128. Gold, "Biographical Sketch."

129. Ibid.

130. Ibid.

131. Ibid.

132. Ibid.; Carrington, lecture notes, 8.

133. Boyd, *Annals and Family Records*, 109.

134. Ibid., 109–11.

135. Ibid., 111; Winchester Center Historical Association newsletter, no. 13 (Summer 2007): 3–6.

136. *Winsted Herald*, "Winchester Center—Fire," August 20, 1875. Theron Bronson's sawmill and cheese box factory, Bronson Family File; Boyd, *Annals and Family Records*, 522.

137. Winchester Institute circular, circa 1859–60, Schools Binder, Beardsley Library.

138. Boyd, *Annals and Family Records*, 528, 617–19.

139. Carrington, lecture notes, 14.

140. Ibid., 16.

141. Boyd, *Annals and Family Records*, 109, 238.

142. Arthur Goodenough, *Clergy of Litchfield County* (Litchfield County University Club, 1909), 88–94.

143. Dwight Whitney Marsh, *Marsh Genealogy 1636–1895* (Amherst, MA: Carpenter & Morehouse, 1895), 215.

144. Carrington, lecture notes, 16.

Chapter 7

145. *Solomon's Temple*, pamphlet (Winsted, CT, 1935), 4, Rockwell Family File, Beardsley Library.

146. June Senack, "Legacy of Solomon Rockwell and His Descendants," *The Voice* (September 1, 1994): 1, 9.

147. *Solomon's Temple*, 4–5; Boyd, *Annals and Family Records*, 618–19.

148. June Senack, "The Story Continues," *The Voice* (September 15, 1994): 8.

149. Ibid., 8–9; Ohio Tax Records, 1800–1850. Available on Ancestry.com when looking for information on Solomon Rockwell.

150. Senack, "Story Continues," 8.

151. Boyd, *Annals and Family Records*, 338.

152. Senack, "Story Continues," 8; Boyd, *Annals and Family Records*, 507–8.

153. Senack, "Story Continues," 8.

154. Ibid., 8–9.
155. Ibid.; Frederick C. Hicks, *Yale Law School: The Founders and the Founders' Collection* (New Haven, CT: Yale University Press, 1935), 13–14.
156. Boyd, *Annals and Family Records*, 316.
157. Senack, "Story Continues," 9.
158. Boyd, *Annals and Family Records*, 316.
159. Ibid., 507–8, 510.
160. Ibid., 436; DeMars and Bronson, *Winsted and the Town of Winchester*, 36, 131.
161. Boyd, *Annals and Family Records*, 617, 619.
162. Ibid., 368. Sadly, the status of women at the time was such that the entry of Delia Ellen Rockwell Beardsley is completely about her husband, Elliot Beardsley. DeMars and Bronson, *Winsted and the Town of Winchester*, 76.
163. DeMars and Bronson, *Winsted and the Town of Winchester*, 76.

Chapter 8

164. Boyd, *Annals and Family Records*, 206, 224.
165. Ibid., 342–43.
166. Ibid., 416–17.
167. Bronson, *New England Village Green*, 16.
168. Ibid., 17.
169. DeMars and Bronson, *Winsted and the Town of Winchester*, 262.
170. Ibid., 262.
171. Ibid., 315.
172. Ibid., 313.
173. Ibid., 263.
174. Horatio T. Strother, *The Underground Railroad in Connecticut* (Middletown, CT: Wesleyan University, 1962), 125.
175. Reverend Samuel Orcutt, *History of Torrington, Conn.* (Albany, NY: J. Munsell, Printer, 1878), 216.
176. Ibid., 217.
177. Ibid.
178. Boyd, *Annals and Family Records*, 309–10.
179. Notes in the Coe Family File, Beardsley Library.
180. Strother, *Underground Railroad*, 125; Boyd, *Annals and Family Records*, 194.
181. Letter from District Attorney William S. Holabird to Secretary of State John Forsyth, mentioned on Famous Trials website, www.famous-trials.com.

182. Holabird Family File, Beardsley Library.
183. *Winsted Herald*, October 28, 1859, 2. All editorials and town news are on the second page of the newspaper.

Chapter 9

184. *Winsted Herald*, "Special Notices," April 19, 1861, 2.
185. Boyd, *Annals and Family Records*, 462–63.
186. Ibid., 463; *Winsted Herald*, "Local Matters," April 19, 1861, 2; *Winsted Herald*, "First Company," April 26, 1861, 1.
187. Boyd, *Annals and Family Records*, 463, 486f. It is noteworthy that Caleb Newman did not make this claim until after Samuel B. Horne moved to Grand Rapids, Michigan, and opened a law office there. It was probably a great surprise when Horne moved back to Winsted and opened a law office. There were at several conflicting stories as to how and when Newman signed up.
188. Ibid., 464; Genealogy in Palmer Family Folder, Beardsley Library.
189. *Winsted Herald*, July 1861, 2.
190. Boyd, *Annals and Family Records*, 464–65.
191. Ibid., 465; *Winsted Herald*, "The Patriotism of the Ladies," May 10, 1861, 2.
192. Boyd, *Annals and Family Records*, 466.
193. *Winsted Herald*, "Soon Home—A Military Funeral," May 17, 1861, 2; *Winsted Herald*, "A Discourse," May 24, 1861, 1.
194. *Winsted Herald*, "Letters from Volunteers," July 19, 1861, 2.
195. *Winsted Herald*, "Capt. Kellogg," June 28, 1861, 2; Boyd, *Annals and Family Records*, 467.
196. Virginia Shultz-Charette, "Rev. Hiram Eddy: The Fighting Parson (1813–1893)," *Winsted Journal*, May 25, 2012, 1, 7; Boyd, *Annals and Family Records*, 467.
197. Shultz-Charette, "Rev. Hiram Eddy," 1, 7.
198. Boyd, *Annals and Family Records*, 467.
199. Ibid., 471.
200. *Winsted Herald*, "A Soldier's Letter," October 10, 1862, 2.
201. Compiled by Authority of the General Assembly, *Record of Service of Connecticut Men in the Army and Navy of the United States During the War of the Rebellion* (Hartford, CT: Case, Lockwood & Brainard Company, 1889), 431, 617.

202. Town of Winchester Mortality Book, Winchester Town Hall. Interestingly, after Coggswell's name is written "colored."

203. Petition Records for William F. Coggswell, filed by his wife, Clairinda, for herself and her recently born child.

204. Encyclopedia Virginia, "Banks, Nathaniel Prentiss (1816–1894)," https://www.encyclopediavirginia.org/Banks_Nathaniel_Prentiss_1816-1894.

205. General Assembly, *Record of Service*, 845.

206. *Winsted Herald*, "The Conn. 28th at Port Hudson—Mark H. Wheeler of Winsted Killed," July 3, 1863.

207. Cornelius Dayton Pension File, released to me by John Banks, who wrote the History Press book *Hidden History of Connecticut Union Soldiers*.

208. John Banks, *Hidden History of Connecticut Union Soldiers* (Charleston, SC: The History Press, 2015), 174–78.

209. Theodore F. Vaill, *History of the Second Connecticut Heavy Artillery* (Winsted, CT: Winsted Printing Company, 1868), 67; Richard Smith, *The Old Nineteenth: The Story of the Second Connecticut Heavy Artillery in the Civil War* (New York: iUniverse Inc.), 132.

210. Smith, *Old Nineteenth*, 2, 4–6, 11–19.

211. Ibid., 29, 44–50, 90–91.

212. Ibid., 106–8.

213. Ibid., 122–23.

214. Ibid., 122–26.

215. Vaill, *History of the Second Connecticut*, 63f; Smith, *Old Nineteenth*, 126–34.

216. Smith, *Old Nineteenth*, 132. Company E, largely comprising Winchester men and led by Captain Jeffrey Skinner, took the highest casualties, which included twenty-nine when missing and presumed dead were added into the totals of those who died on that day and those who were mortally wounded. A little less than half were from Winchester/Winsted.

217. In the library's Samuel Horne Family Folder, there is a loose article, just dated 1926, that gives Horne's description of what he suffered at Cold Harbor from his two wounds.

218. Transcripts of Tuttle Civil War letters, Tuttle Family Folder, Beardsley Library.

219. Smith, *Old Nineteenth*, 215–17; Vaill, *History of the Second Connecticut*, 130.

220. Smith, *Old Nineteenth*, 218–19, 233–35.

221. *Winsted Herald*, August 8, 1862, 2.

222. Ibid.

223. *Winsted Herald*, December 12, 1862, 2.

224. The Descendents of the 29th Regiment, "Soldier Stories," http://www.conn29th.org/stories.htm.

225. W.F. Beyer and O.F. Keydel, *Deeds of Valor: How American's Civil War Heroes Won the Congressional Medal of Honor* (New York: Smithmark Publishers, 2000), 433–34.

226. William Richard Cutter, AM, *New England Families, Genealogical and Memorial* (New York: Lewis Historical Publishing Company, 1913), 1,162–63; Connecticut History, "The 29th Regiment Connecticut Volunteer Infantry Flag & Display," www.connecticuthistory.org.

Chapter 10

227. Boyd, *Annals and Family Records*, 438.

228. DeMars and Bronson, *Winsted and the Town of Winchester*, 28.

229. *History of Litchfield County, Connecticut* (Philadelphia, PA: J.W. Lewis & Company, 1881), 222.

230. Ibid., 227.

231. Mary W. Pitt, "Park Cottage—Home of William H. Phelps, 1852," *Winsted Voice*, House Binder, Beardsley Library.

232. Boyd, *Annals and Family Records*, 454.

233. DeMars and Bronson, *Winsted and the Town of Winchester*, 265–68.

234. Ibid., 290–96.

235. Boyd, *Annals and Family Records*, 491–92.

236. Ibid., 617; DeMars and Bronson, *Winsted and the Town of Winchester*, 65.

237. DeMars and Bronson, *Winsted and the Town of Winchester*, 71.

238. *History of Litchfield County*, 227–28.

239. Ibid., 230.

240. DeMars and Bronson, *Winsted and the Town of Winchester*, 105; Virginia Shultz-Charette and Verna Gilson, *Winsted and Winchester*, Images of America series (Charleston, SC: Arcadia Publishing, 2012), 51.

241. Strong Family Folder, Beardsley Library.

242. Strong Manufacturing/Walnut Street Tour, June 18, 2016.

243. DeMars *Winsted*, 99, 152.

244. Ibid., 110; *Hartford Courant*, "Jay E. Spaulding Dies as Result of Fall: Was President of New England Pin Co.," January 7, 1911, 2; *Winsted Tercentenarian*, "The Winsted Hosiery, the New England Knitting Mills," August 1, 1935, 63.

245. DeMars and Bronson, *Winsted and the Town of Winchester*, 122–23.

246. Ibid., 70.

247. Ibid., 104; William Davis Godman, Inez Godman and A.H. Dexter Godman, *Gilbert Academy and Agricultural College, Winsted, Louisiana: Sketches and Incidents* (New York: Hunt & Eaton, 1893).

248. Soldiers' Monument and Memorial Park website, http://www.soldiersmonumenttwinsted.org/monument-history.html.

249. *Hartford Courant*, "She Let Her Light Shine," February 12, 1892, 6.

250. DeMars and Bronson, *Winsted and the Town of Winchester*, 125–26; Joseph A. O'Brien, "The Life and Times of Local Benefactress Susan Perry," *Winsted Journal*, November 6, 1998, Brown Family Folder, Beardsley Library.

251. DeMars and Bronson, *Winsted and the Town of Winchester*, 126; Shultz-Charette and Gilson, *Winsted and Winchester*, 122–23.

252. DeMars and Bronson, *Winsted and the Town of Winchester*, 126, 171; Shultz-Charette and Gilson, *Winsted and Winchester*, 124.

253. *Evening Citizen*, "William L. Gilbert, Town Benefactor," April 3, 1939, 6–7.

254. "Gilbert Home, 50 Years Old, Haven of Youth," William L. Gilbert Family Folder.

Chapter 11

255. DeMars and Bronson, *Winsted and the Town of Winchester*, 27.

256. Ibid., 39–40.

257. *Hartford Courant*, "Cool Stuff," January 23, 1994, H1–H8.

258. Patricia Carter Magee, "The Icehouses," in *Highland Lake Reflections* (Winsted, CT: Highland Lake Watershed Association, 2010), 188–94.

259. DeMars and Bronson, *Winsted and the Town of Winchester*, 40.

260. Magee, "Icehouses," 192–94.

261. DeMars and Bronson, *Winsted and the Town of Winchester*, 301.

262. Ibid., 302–3.

263. Highland Transportation Company, *A Day's Outing by Rail and Water, Season 1890*, brochure.

264. Shultz-Charette and Gilson, *Winsted and Winchester*, 30–32.

265. DeMars and Bronson, *Winsted and the Town of Winchester*, 195.

266. Ibid., 303, 308; Shultz-Charette and Gilson, *Winsted and Winchester*, 37, 38.

267. DeMars and Bronson, *Winsted and the Town of Winchester*, 308, 310; Shultz-Charette and Gilson, *Winsted and Winchester*, 40.

268. DeMars and Bronson, *Winsted and the Town of Winchester*, 310.

269. Highland Transportation Company, *Day's Outing*.

Chapter 12

270. DeMars and Bronson, *Winsted and the Town of Winchester*, 95–96.

271. Ibid., 339.

272. Jean Downey, "A Biographical and Critical Study of Rose Terry Cooke" (diss., University of Ottawa, 1956), 41. Downey also noted that Rose Terry was a direct descendant of Joseph Wadsworth, the man who allegedly stole the charter, and Daniel Wadsworth, who for a number of years sent Rose Terry a small stipend so that she could write. Unfortunately, the stipend eventually ran out, which imperiled Rose Terry Cook's financial ability to support her family.

273. DeMars and Bronson, *Winsted and the Town of Winchester*, 338.

274. Ibid., 337; Rose Terry Cooke, "An Old-Fashioned Thanksgiving," *Huckleberries: Gathered from New England Hills* (n.p.: Bibliolife, 2010), 122–51. Jean Downey mistakenly characterized this story as set during the Civil War. However, the initials G.W., cocked hat and Continental dollars dictate that the true period is that of the Revolutionary War.

275. Ibid., DeMars, 338.

276. Princeton University Art Museum catalogue, copy at Beardsley Library.

277. Melissa Jordan-Reilly, "Winsted Folk Artist to Be Celebrated," *Winsted Journal*, May 2, 2003, section Art 1.

278. *Winsted Evening Citizen*, "Article on Life of Sarah E. Harvey Produced in Script," May 10, 1966, 9.

279. Princeton University Art Museum catalogue.

280. DeMars and Bronson, *Winsted and the Town of Winchester*, 329.

281. Ibid., 330; Historic Camera, http://historiccamera.com.

282. Robert McNamara, "Stereographs and Stereoscopes," ThoughtCo, updated May 1, 2018, https://www.thoughtco.com/stereographs-and-stereoscopes-1773924.

283. DeMars and Bronson, *Winsted and the Town of Winchester*, 331.

284. Ibid., 331–32.

285. Ibid., 332.

286. Alfred E. Moore, "Amateur Ballooning," *Century Magazine* (1886): 672–76.

287. John G. Doughty, "Balloon Experiences of a Timid Photographer," *Century Magazine* (1886): 680.

288. Ibid., 679–93.

289. Bowery Boys: New York City History, "Lots of Hot Air: Joseph Pulitzer's Failed Balloon Stunt," www.boweryboyshistory.com.

290. Oral history at the Colebrook Historical Society, February 22, 1989, interviewer Cynthia Baldwin. Discussed the life and career of Frank DeMars with his daughter, Martha Ruth DeMars Richards.

291. Sylvia Whitman, "Mattie Ruth Cross," Handbook of Texas Online, www.tshaonline.org/handbook/entries/cross-mattie-ruth. All biographical content outside of Winsted comes from this source.

292. Ruth Cross, *Eden On a Country Hill* (New York: H.C. Kinsey & Company, 1938), 6.

293. DeMars and Bronson, *Winsted and the Town of Winchester*, 326.

294. The Louis T. Stone scrapbook, donated by Norma Thomsen and Jean Prindle to the Beardsley Library Collection, contains numerous articles, accolades and obituary notices for the "Winsted Liar," whose tall tales circled the world.

295. The bridge was removed when the dry dam was built.

Chapter 13

296. *New York Times*, "Use of Deceptive Labels Forbidden," April 25, 1922.

297. Boyd, *Annals and Family Records*, 443–44.

298. Ibid., 498.

299. Barreuther Family Folder, Beardsley Library.

300. *Winsted Sentinel*, vol. 1, February 1908, 1.

301. David Rivera, "Dry? Never, to Hear Winsteders Tell of Prohibition," *Country Journal*, January 18, 2003, 1B–2B.

302. Virginia Shultz-Charette, "Past Is Prologue: Winsted and the 1918 Spanish Flu Epidemic," *Winsted Phoenix*, May 7, 2020, 10.

303. DeMars and Bronson, *Winsted and the Town of Winchester*, 201, 213.

304. Ibid., 201.

305. Ibid., 219.

306. Ibid., 223. This addendum to the book was added by Elliott P. Bronson after DeMars's death.

307. Beardsley and Memorial Library Genealogy and Local History Room, *"Brains, Money & Pluck": Profiles of Early Industries, Winsted Connecticut* (Torrington, CT: Print Master, 2014), 47–48.

308. Ibid., 48.

309. DeMars and Bronson, *Winsted and the Town of Winchester*, 223.

310. Ibid.

311. Ibid., 224.

312. Ibid., 160, 163.

313. George Sherwood and Sarah Tryon, "In Winsted the Post Office Moves Fast: A History of Post Office Locations in Winchester/Winsted," *Winsted Voice*, undated, page 5.

314. Boyd, *Annals and Family Records*, 431–33. Boyd claimed that to not discuss the post office in Winsted would be "like performing the play *Hamlet* with Hamlet himself left out."

315. DeMars and Bronson, *Winsted and the Town of Winchester*, 132.

316. Ibid., 214.

317. The Cornelio Legacy Film, July 6, 2009, available at www.winsted 1948.com.

Chapter 14

318. *Evening Citizen*, "Civil Defense Issues Warning on Hurricanes," August 9, 1955, 1.

319. *Evening Citizen*, "Hurricane Slowing Threatens to Swing on Connie's Course," undated, 1.

320. William G. Hoyd and Walter Landgren, *Floods* (Princeton, NJ: Princeton University Press, 1955); David M. Ludton, *American Hurricanes: 1492–1870* (n.p.: American Meteorological Society, 1963). In a program I did for the Beardsley Library on the 1955 flood in June 2005, I used these sources to develop a chart of probable hurricanes in Winsted.

321. DeMars and Bronson, *Winsted and the Town of Winchester*, 33. Other flood mentions are found in the Beardsley Library flood archives, often undated.

322. *Evening Citizen*, "Serious Floods Menace Section, Waters Block Several Highways, Property Damage Believed Heavy," March 12, 1936, 1.

323. *Evening Citizen*, "Winsted Passes through Most Disastrous Flood in History," September 22, 1938, 1.

324. *Register Citizen*, "Timeline," 1995.

325. John Hersey, "A Reporter at Large: Over the Mad River," *New Yorker*, October 1955, 121–22.

326. Ted Zoli, "Winsted, Connecticut, Highland Lake, 1947–1959," *Reflections*, Highland Lake Watershed, 79–80.

327. Hersey, "Reporter at Large," 123.

328. Flood Binders, Beardsley Archives.

329. DeMars and Bronson, *Winsted and the Town of Winchester*, 227; Beardsley and Memorial Library Genealogy and Local History Room, *"Brains,"* 37.
330. DeMars and Bronson, *Winsted and the Town of Winchester*, 228.
331. Senate Public Appropriations Hearing, 1958—Benefits of Dry Dam, 1,070, as well as letter from Howd, 1,071.

ABOUT THE AUTHOR

Virginia Shultz-Charette is a graduate of the University of Massachusetts–Amherst, where she specialized in Civil War history, women's political history and public history. She is a member of the Winchester Soldiers' Monument Commission, dedicated to maintaining the Civil War monument, which is in the National Register of Historic Places. She has given numerous programs about the war and the more than three hundred soldiers listed on the monument. She has also given walking tours, done research for the monument's annual cemetery walks and written a book with Verna Gilson for Arcadia's Images of America series about Winsted and Winchester. She lives with her husband, her youngest son and her cocker spaniel, Tobey.